Instructions

LET AUGMENTED REALITY CH/

With your smartphone, iPad or tablet you can use the **Hasmark AR** app to invoke the augmented reality experience to literally read outside the book.

 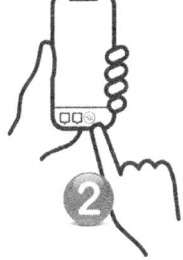 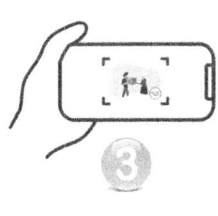

1. Download the **Hasmark app** from the **Apple App Store** or **Google Play**

2. Open and select the (vue) option

3. Point your lens at the full image with the and enjoy the augmented reality experience.

Go ahead and try it right now with the Hasmark Publishing International logo.

"Immerse Yourself in Transformation with 'The Remembering Technique' by Donna Laine! Step into a world of endless possibilities as Donna Laine guides you through a journey of self-discovery and empowerment. 'The Remembering Technique' isn't just a book—it's a roadmap to reshaping your future and crafting the life you've always dreamed of.

With a wealth of positive techniques, practical antidotes, and expert advice, Laine empowers readers to script and manifest their desired events, relationships, and circumstances effortlessly. Through relatable stories and vivid examples, she illustrates the power of visualization and 'Remembering' in sculpting an ideal reality. Laine's warm and encouraging tone makes each page a joy to read, infusing the journey with a sense of possibility and optimism. Highly recommended for your reading list!"

~ A.M.Egan
Author of *Tune Into Wellness, Tune Into Intuition*

"'The Remembering Technique' by Donna Laine is an empowering guide to self-discovery and understanding The Laws of Attraction. Through her personal experiences, Donna has written a captivating book with practical advice and guidance to help her reader understand the Remembering Technique and to apply it to day to day life."

~ Nancy Duval
International Bestselling author of
Whispers From Beyond

"Author Donna Laine is a true force with her transformational book 'The Remembering Technique.' The pages of this book will encourage you to embrace and integrate this powerful technique into your daily life. Donna weaves personal anecdotes with guiding practices to help you on your journey to fully utilizing The Remembering Technique."

~ Judy O'Beirn
President of **Hasmark Publishing International**

THE REMEMBERING
TECHNIQUE™

by
DONNA LAINE

Editor: Brad Green (brad@hasmarkpublishing.com
Cover Design: Anne Karklins (anne@hasmarkpublishing.com)
Interior Layout: Amit Dey (amit@hasmarkpublishing.com)

ISBN 13: 978-1-77482-297-5
ISBN 10: 1-77482-297-0

DEDICATION

Thank you to the main people that have inspired me, supported me, and believed in me.

To my daughter, Willow, who teaches me as much as I teach her. You are a joy. You are wise, and you are beautiful inside and out. I love you.

Nick, my love, my life, my rock.

Peggy, my friend and mentor, who believed in me and this book unconditionally, who kept me on track and on time. You were an inspiration before I met you, and working with you has been continuously inspiring. You are an incredible spirit, and I am proud to call you my friend.

FOREWORD FROM PEGGY MCCOLL

In the vast library of my life, filled with the wisdom of thousands of volumes, there comes along, once in a rare while, a book that does more than occupy shelf space—it nestles itself in the very nooks of my heart. Donna Laine's *The Remembering Technique* is such a treasure, a work that stands out in its uniqueness and efficacy.

Since January 1979, personal development has been the compass by which I navigate, a passion that led to the inception of my personal and professional development business in December 1994. Along this journey, and up to this point in my life, I've authored 23 books, each a stepping stone in the art of manifestation—a subject I've not only taught but lived.

Donna's masterpiece, however, is a refreshing departure from the trodden path. It's an odyssey that begins with the end—a celebration of achievements yet to come. It's an invitation to dance with your future self, to embrace your dreams with a warmth that turns aspiration into reality.

Her book is not just a read; it's an experience. It whispers the possibility of a life where you're no longer a scribe to past events but the creator of your narrative. Donna invites you to paint your destiny with bold strokes of intention and purpose, where the mundane becomes magical, and the simple act of remembering transforms into the alchemy of achievement.

I stand in admiration of Donna's work, which aligns so closely with my own teachings yet illuminates an entirely new dimension. *The Remembering Technique* is a testament to the untapped power within us all, a gentle guide that leads to the realization of what we've always desired but perhaps never believed possible.

As you turn the pages, may you find the echoes of your own dreams and the courage to manifest them. This is not just another book; it's a journey into the heart of what makes us truly alive—the relentless pursuit of a life crafted by our deepest longings.

May this book be your gateway to a future you remember fondly before it unfolds, a future that you, from this moment on, have the joy and privilege to design.

With heartfelt enthusiasm,

Peggy McColl, *New York Times* Best-Selling Author
http://PeggyMcColl.com

A few words from Donna Laine

With a passion to learn and try new things, I embarked on a life of trial and error that crafted the person I am today.

Strong words from the young, red-headed girl who endured bullying and often felt left out, daydreaming amongst the trees as she gazed out the school window.

These formative years instilled in me a sense of determination and an unwavering focus on creating a better life for my miracle daughter.

My journey has been fortunate enough to lead me through the realms of self-development, a journey filled with both joy and disappointment. It was a path I couldn't seem to fully harness. I've delved into various techniques and experienced a wide array of outcomes, always progressing, yet never quite realizing the entirety of my dreams.

Now, the time has come to unlock unprecedented levels of success, all thanks to this straightforward and unforgettable technique.

I feel privileged to be a part of your new journey because I know that *The Remembering Technique* works and will continue to work in countless ways. You are now the master of your own destiny.

Lots of love,
Donna Laine
xxx

TABLE OF CONTENTS

Chapter One

EMBRACING YOUR
FUTURE NOW

Welcome to a transformative journey that begins in a distinctive and unconventional manner, strategically crafted to maximize your engagement and unlock the full potential of this book.

As we embark on this shared journey, embrace the dual roles of being an active participant and a keen observer and witness to the unfolding of your desires.

Imagine yourself at the culmination of this book, a subtle yet confident smile adorning your lips, as if a weighty and profound secret has been lifted from your shoulders. You now know the secret to manifesting your most profound desires.

This book serves as a vessel for time travel, a means by which you can project yourself into the future and savor the outcomes you desire as if they have already materialized.

Your curiosity has led you to this moment, a pivotal juncture where the canvas of your life eagerly awaits your artistic touch. The colors you choose, the scenes you paint, all lie within your control.

For too long, you've played the role of an archivist, diligently cataloging the events of the past. Now, it's time to step into the role of an architect, applying the same effortless recall to your tomorrows as you do to your yesterdays.

Think of your life as a narrative, a tapestry woven from the repetition of memories, interpretations of moments both joyous and challenging. These memories, shaped by external influences and circumstances, have guided your journey. But what if, starting today, you could reverse this paradigm? Envision having the power to shape your destiny—choosing the relationships, career, and lifestyle that align with your true essence.

Why limit your mental prowess to mundane tasks like memorizing shopping lists or birthdays? Why not employ this innate capacity to envision and, in doing so, craft a brighter future?

You have stumbled upon the world's most closely guarded secret, a technique so elegantly simple and profoundly transformative that its discovery marks a new era in personal empowerment. This technique is as effective and limitless as the horizon, granting you the privilege of handpicking your own destiny.

Remember:

This book transcends mere pages; it serves as a gateway to potential—an innate potential as fundamental as your very breath.

In the voyage of life, decisions act as our guiding rudders. Dare to embrace change. Start with small steps, relish the incremental victories, and use them as the foundation for your journey.

What commences as a faint whisper of transformation will inevitably crescendo into a symphony of success.

This technique is not just a theoretical concept; it's a tried-and-true path to fulfillment. It has paved the way to achieving my dream home, finding a loving partner, and attaining professional triumphs.

Allow it to be the bridge to your own aspirations as well.

You need not blindly believe; simply grant this method an opportunity. Experiment with it, engage in the process, and let your personal experiences be the ultimate judge.

Chapter Two

THE INCEPTION
OF A NEW PERSPECTIVE

2017 marked the beginning of a transformative journey.

Chapter Two of our journey delves into a foundational aspect of self-awareness and responsibility within the transformative practice of remembering.

As we set forth on this path, it becomes crucial to first ground ourselves in the present moment—to gain a clear understanding of our current position in our lives.

This chapter is dedicated to exploring the vital significance of recognizing our present state, not as a constraint but as a launching point for personal growth and change. It's about transitioning from a reactive stance, often entangled in blame and passivity, to a proactive mindset that embraces full responsibility for our life experiences.

Here, we uncover how this shift not only empowers us but also aligns our remembering practices with our genuine aspirations. This alignment sets the stage for authentic transformation and paves the way to success.

How did this innovative approach emerge?

After years of experimenting with the Law of Attraction and achieving modest success, I often found myself pondering a fundamental question: "Can this process be simplified?" Despite my best efforts, consistency often eluded me, with life's complexities frequently getting in the way. I dabbled in various methodologies, enough to fill a book about their efficacy. Yet, one mantra guided me: The past should not dictate the future.

While my experiences with the Law of Attraction had been positive, I sensed there was room for a more effortless approach.

My story unfolds:

This technique crystallized during a tumultuous phase when I was a single parent, seeking to escape a toxic relationship. My daughter and I found refuge in a rented three-story house, a sanctuary amid the chaos of our lives. My young daughter claimed the third floor as her own, a bedroom and bathroom that offered her a semblance of peace.

In our new home, I felt an overwhelming sense of gratitude for liberating myself from my previous marriage, and my daughter, too, found joy in this new chapter of our lives. However, one Sunday evening, as I prepared dinner and she ran a bath, our tranquility was shattered. Water cascaded down the stairs from an overflowing bathtub, leaving its aftermath on all three floors. That night was a challenge, but with the support of friends, we persevered despite the lack of electricity, water, and heating.

The incident left unsightly stains on the ceilings, and the cost to repaint them was beyond my financial means. So, I took it upon myself to tackle the task. As I painted, an audiobook on music composition played in the background. In that moment, a thought struck me: If musicians could recall tunes, could I "remember" the future? Could altering my memories shape my reality?

I scoured the internet in search of similar concepts but found none. Undeterred, I embarked on this novel idea by starting to write diary entries from a future perspective. These entries weren't mere predictions; they were memories crafted in advance. I experimented with different formats, including letters and diary entries, and noticed that the most profound impact came from those written in the diary. Gradually, I extended my foresight, writing about aspects like health, events, and financial goals—crucial considerations for a single parent with no support from an ex-husband.

It all began with a deceptively simple idea: Why not write to my future self? Although this had been done before, I was about to embark on a unique journey with it—the Remembering Technique.

I sat down with a diary and began to write about the day I desired in the future, writing as if it had already occurred. It felt good; it felt right. I had tried various methods, including letters from my future self to my present self, but I found the diary entries to be the most engaging and effective.

I started with writing a week in advance, then extended it to ten days, and eventually dared to plan a month into the future. I experimented with various scenarios, ranging from health to events and financial goals. Money was a particularly crucial aspect of my life as a single parent, and I was determined to make my new life work. The question that hung in the air was whether this novel idea would truly work.

To my amazement, things began to shift. My small jewelry shop, which I had established with my late mother's inheritance, experienced an unprecedented wave of success. I had always been a skilled salesperson, but this was different. My new approach transformed customer interactions and boosted sales. The shop's ambiance shifted, and I felt as if I were soaring.

Encouraged by this success, I expanded the technique to all facets of my life. I "remembered" fantastic holidays, smooth travel experiences, and ideal outcomes. When I had penned these entries, I only reviewed them once for their fulfillment. The results were astonishing: seamless trips, enjoyable vacations, and newfound serenity and confidence.

Allow me to share an example of how I remembered a splendid future holiday. In my diary, I meticulously scripted my journey with ease and flow, expressing my joy as if it had already happened. I then let it go and never revisited it until my return. The outcome was remarkable: no traffic jams, no airport troubles, flights were punctual, seats were perfect, and the holiday unfolded exactly as I had envisioned. It felt effortless, and I had never experienced such calmness, serenity, and happiness. I felt lighter and happier, simply enjoying the moment and finding solutions instead of problems.

While life may not always be perfect, I vividly remember taking my daughter and nephew skiing, all on my own. I employed the Remembering Technique to envision my holiday and everything I desired to happen. The journey was extraordinary, the ski resort exceeded my expectations, and everything I had "remembered" came to fruition. One picturesque day while skiing, I encountered a patch of hard ice on a ski run and suffered a significant knee injury. I was skiing with my nephew at the time, but incredibly, I remembered my technique of envisioning things working out with ease and flow (which is why I write and am happy today—it infuses a positive spin on life's events).

A doctor appeared seemingly out of nowhere and provided immediate assistance. He called the rescue service, who swiftly evacuated me from the mountain. Remarkably, there was no charge, as is often the case in Italy. They arranged for an ambulance, collected my daughter from ski school, and we headed to the hospital.

Throughout this ordeal, I continued to remember that everything was going to be okay. At the hospital, an English volunteer kindly assisted with the children, my doctor spoke English, and my treatment proceeded smoothly. Eventually, I was transported back to the resort by ambulance. While my knee was injured and placed in a soft cast, there was still much to be grateful for.

We were nearing the end of our holiday, and remarkably, no time was lost. I contacted the insurance company, and they organized our return flight with complete assistance for me and the children, all at no cost. Several seats were booked to accommodate my leg and ensure my comfort. It may not have been a perfect holiday, but it turned out much better than I could have ever anticipated.

The essence of this technique lies in repetition. Remember, you have the power to choose, and what you invest in this practice is what you will reap. Be patient with yourself and the outcomes. They will manifest just as you remember them or even better.

Remind yourself that you possess the knowledge and skill to do this. Now, can you apply it to shape your future?

To move forward, we must undergo change—it's a fundamental aspect of your new life. You cannot create something different by adhering to the same beliefs, actions, or behaviors. If you genuinely aspire to live the life of your dreams, you must first understand where you presently stand and take full responsibility for it. This isn't about self-criticism; it's a straightforward way to gain awareness of your current situation.

Approach this without judgment or regret. It happened, and you are where you are. Acknowledge it and make the decision to move forward, enabling you to implement the changes you need to make. When you look back from your new life, you'll appreciate how far you've come.

Summary – Achieving Clarity and Taking Responsibility

1. **Recognizing Your Current State:** The path to a successful life through the art of remembering starts with understanding where you are now. Acknowledge and accept your current circumstances. This awareness is the first step in moving towards a culture of success instead of blame.

2. **Embracing Responsibility for Personal Growth:** Taking responsibility for your current situation is an empowering step. It means recognizing not only your accomplishments but also areas that require improvement. This shift in mindset is essential for personal growth and lays the foundation for effectively using the Remembering Technique.

3. **The Importance of Daily Commitment:** Commit to this daily practice. It's not a one-time endeavor but an ongoing journey of self-awareness and personal growth. Keep in mind that this technique is more than just a tool; it's a way of life centered around consistently comprehending and molding your identity, your possessions, and your aspirations.

4. **Transforming Blame into Proactive Success:** Shifting away from blame, whether directed at circumstances or others, is the key to unlocking the potential of remembering. When you assume responsibility for your life, you acquire the ability to transform it. Utilize this

newfound power to shape a more positive and successful future.

5. **Realizing the Power of Your Current Position:** Comprehending your present circumstances enables you to establish practical and attainable goals. It involves harmonizing your Remembering Techniques with your real-life situation, thereby creating the foundation for authentic transformation and success.

6. **Daily Remembering:** Integrate daily remembering exercises that encompass both your current situation and your envisioned future. This routine reinforces your dedication to personal growth and transformation.

7. **Reflecting on Past Experiences for Growth:** Leverage your past experiences as learning opportunities for personal growth. Reflecting on these moments offers valuable insights that can inform your present and future remembering exercises.

In conclusion, this entire chapter merges the principles of self-awareness, responsibility, and daily dedication with the hands-on implementation of the Remembering Technique. This chapter serves as a guide to comprehending your present circumstances and leveraging this awareness as the cornerstone for personal development and achievement. It underscores the significance of assuming responsibility for your life and utilizing the technique of remembering as a means to reshape your present and craft your desired future.

Chapter Three

WHAT WILL YOU NEED?

Remember to use these tools, don't forget.

Chapter Three invites us on a journey aimed at clarifying and articulating our deepest desires—a pivotal step in unlocking the power of remembering.

Within this chapter, we delve into the transformative practice of redirecting our focus away from the burdens of what we wish to avoid, and instead, towards the empowering clarity of our true aspirations. It's a journey that transcends the cycle of negative thoughts and complaints, replacing them with a precise and positive vision of what we genuinely long for.

Through this new perspective, we discover how to redefine our future, harnessing the power of our intentions to mold experiences and outcomes that align with our core ambitions.

This chapter serves as a guide to utilizing the art of remembering as both a tool for introspection and a beacon that illuminates the path to realizing our most cherished goals.

What tools will you need?

- Discipline
- Commitment
- A clear outline/goal of what you want to achieve.
- A journal – Go to my website and download your free the Remembering Technique Journal.

Instead of a journal, you could also use a diary. (I recommend an academic diary; it spans the new year dateline and allows the mind and linear thinking to let go.) Go to my website and download the Remembering Technique Diary.

Write a letter to yourself, a friend, or a family member, reminiscing about a wonderful time. I adore letter writing and sharing my world through it, as it allows others to enjoy the story with me. Letters have a unique quality—they invite revisiting, ensuring the story is enjoyed repeatedly.

Memory cards are another tool I use daily. Recall specific moments by asking, 'Remember when... You did this or that.' These cards will help you remember future dates and can serve as prompts or scripts for voice recordings.

Whether through journaling, diary entries, or letter writing, these methods add depth to your journey of remembering.

Now that you know what you want and where you're headed, how do you make this journey easier?

Number 1: Journal

Acquire a blank journal and inscribe your aspirations. Over time, I've explored various methods of remembering, but it consistently circles back to this: I remember with such clarity, ease, and joy that I experienced the best day ever, where everything seamlessly fell into place.

You can employ this practice either at the start of your day or the evening prior, visualizing your day ahead.

I shared this technique with a friend who was aiming for her dream job (which she achieved with this technique), one that posed fresh challenges, including a new colleague. I suggested she start remembering a positive outcome for both of them. She practiced remembering the night before a crucial meeting, envisioning everything working out favorably for both parties, with all issues resolved for their mutual benefit.

The following day, she reached out to me with boundless enthusiasm. The meeting had unfolded precisely as she had remembered it—pleasant, constructive, and filled with positivity, surpassing her expectations.

In your journal, you can inscribe: Don't forget what an exceptional day it was. Everything flowed perfectly, and I remember feeling happy, serene, and triumphant. I effortlessly navigated through it all, and the harmony was palpable. We all basked in contentment and enjoyed a fantastic time together."

You can write this:

- A week in advance
- 10 days in advance
- A month in advance
- 3 months in advance
- A year in advance
- 3 years in advance

There is no limit to your future. Keep in mind that both you and life evolve as you achieve these changes, and your wants and desires will naturally shift. Stay flexible but specific, ensuring that you don't inadvertently impose limits on yourself in the future.

Number 2: Diary

Buy a diary. We typically use diaries to organize our lives, jog our memories for appointments and birthdays, and generally help manage our day-to-day affairs. But here's where we take a different approach. Instead of using diaries for the usual organizational purposes, we employ this technique within our everyday schedule. It's so straightforward that you can implement it not only days, weeks, or months in advance but even mere hours before an event.

Now, which diary should you choose? I've tried various options and prefer the A5 academic diary, mainly because it spans the transition from Christmas to New Year, ensuring a seamless flow in your practice.If you're eager to learn more, there are numerous ways to utilize your diary effectively:

You can jot down your desired outcomes or goals for various timeframes—5 years, 3 years, 12 months, 6 months, 3 months, 1 month, 2 weeks, 10 days, a week, or even just a day. There are no limits, and it's essential to bear in mind that you will undergo changes as your life unfolds.

A critical caveat when envisioning your future is to think big. Do not limit yourself to your current circumstances. You are leaving your current reality behind; your diary is the magic wand you've been seeking! As you step into your new life, you will undergo transformation, and you'll never be the same again.

Change is imperative to achieve the results you desire. As the saying goes, "If you always do what you've always done, you'll always get what you've always got." Keep in mind that we often tend to overestimate what we can accomplish in a year and underestimate what we can achieve in 5 years. What if you could expedite that process? Be gentle with yourself, and allow it to unfold naturally.

Number 3: Handwriting or typing?

Don't forget that you have the option to type a journal or diary of your remembering. Writing holds immense power in manifesting your desires. When you articulate your aspirations on paper, in a book, or on a digital platform and then recall them effortlessly, you engage in constructive self-dialogue. Writing, in any format, serves as a means of gaining clarity and interpreting what you truly want.

In the old days, when you affixed your signature or mark, you inscribed your name or symbol onto paper, and it was believed to invoke a kind of spell. In a way, it did; this is why we have the term "spellings," which originated from the days when we crafted spells. Now is the perfect moment to create your own new spells.

Another noteworthy example is the continued use of wet ink, such as a ballpoint pen or ink pen, in legal documents, contracts, or agreements; it holds binding significance. Utilizing wet ink commits you to your desire, aligning with how you've remembered it. In essence, you're crafting your own personal contract with yourself.

Think in ink. It works.

Number 4: Writing a Letter

This practice is truly enjoyable, as it reminds us of the joy that comes with receiving a letter—whether it arrives in the post, is delivered by hand, or simply received with love.

Love letters have been written for centuries, and it appears that love expressed on paper endures, just as your letter will endure for you. It's a delightful endeavor that I embrace wholeheartedly. I write to myself, my daughter, and even my late mom. (This practice allows me to maintain a connection with her, as if she were still here. Because of my emotional bond with my mother, it infuses the act of remembering with deeper significance.)

Here's a letter I recently wrote:

(Remember, I always assume I'm in the future when reminiscing about the day.)

January 15, 2024

Dear Mum (or Donna, Uncle, Aunt, Dad, Nick, or whomever you choose—I chose my mum today),

I just wanted to drop you a line and catch up. It's been quite eventful in recent weeks, and we're all doing well, eagerly looking forward to summer. Christmas was amazing. The shop exceeded all expectations, and Willow had an extraordinary skiing holiday. She was thrilled to be with her friends, and her skiing skills have improved significantly. It's amazing how the lessons at the dry ski slope paid off. Even after three years without skiing, she remains a confident and skilled skier.

The shop shattered all its sales records for December, and the Christmas market was an absolute delight. The weather was dry and cold, and we had the pleasure of serving numerous wonderful customers. I must say, I thoroughly enjoyed it. The stall looked stunning, and we had the right merchandise at the right prices.

Our holiday in Italy was nothing short of brilliant—the best we've had. We made a quick trip to Limone; do you remember Limone? What a fantastic resort it is. The journey was smooth and timely, our accommodations were perfect, and we relished every moment. It was a perfect escape after the bustling Christmas season. We were all calm, serene, and filled with happiness.

That's all for now, Mum. I look forward to sharing more updates soon.

With love,

Donna xxx

Number 5: Voice Recording

Voice recording what you've written and replaying it repeatedly can be highly effective. I personally use the Voice Memos app on my iPhone, a simple yet handy tool. I've crafted a script for remembering my future; it can be concise, but I typically create recordings lasting between 3 and 6 minutes. Here's an example:

"It comes naturally to me to remember that I am efficient and organized. I remember that I enjoy the very best in life. I remember to welcome everything with ease and happiness. I remember that the right solutions arrive at the perfect moment. I remember that my life is truly wonderful. I remember that I consistently make excellent decisions for myself. I remember that life is a breeze. I remember that I sleep soundly. I remember to appreciate every aspect of who I am. I remember to be kind to myself. I remember that I have the very best."

Below is a testament to remembering something quite simple but effective for me.

I recently stumbled upon a recording from 2019 that I had stored on my iPhone's voice memos. On that particular day, I was grappling with the task of dressing my shop window and managing my paperwork—an aspect I'm not particularly fond of.

I often listen to books on Audible, CDs, or even cassettes (which may reveal my age). I decided to record and play my future remembering before heading to work. The impact was astounding. Dressing the window became a joyful, effortless endeavor, and the results were appealing. I went on to have an outstanding day in sales and efficiently completed all my paperwork. It was an unforgettable day, marked by ease and simplicity.

The recording was a mere 3 minutes in duration, unburdened and enjoyable. And the best part is, you can do this too!

The essence of this practice is the fun of it. All you need to do is remember to transport yourself into the future and look back. For instance:

You can specify an exact date, or opt for a more general approach, such as "January 2023." I remember with crystal clarity and absolute certainty how effortlessly December 2022 unfolded. It was a month filled with joy, and everything fell into place harmoniously in all aspects of my life. We exceeded last year's sales target and had an incredible time doing it, thanks to our delightful customers and very happy money.

Christmas was an absolute delight; all of us radiated happiness and contentment. It felt effortless. January, in turn, surpassed even my wildest expectations. We embraced health, happiness, and success. We secured our dream house, bidding farewell to the old one with remarkable ease. The place looked stunning, and we found delighted buyers for our surplus furniture. Transitioning to our new home was seamless and exhilarating. Our new furniture arrived on time, and it was nothing short of extraordinary. We were overjoyed at how smoothly everything fell into place, culminating in our successful completion on January 20th. We did it!

Moving into our lucky, happy, beautiful house was an experience filled with gladness, and our neighbors are simply wonderful. Remarkably, we achieved this feat in one of the most challenging mortgage markets. The situation was exacerbated by Liz Truss's radical budget, which sent shockwaves through the market. Mortgage products were withdrawn, interest rates surged, and we had six mortgage offers revoked without explanation.

However, I persevered, diligently playing my recorded affirmations and exploring every idea that crossed my mind. It wasn't easy, especially given the emotional toll of wanting to leave our rented house desperately. Now, I proudly manage my digital mortgage through a user-friendly app. The process turned out to be remarkably smooth. I applied, provided the requested information, witnessed surveyors' visits, and monitored every step through my app. It unfolded precisely as I remembered it, and by January 2023, our dream home had become a reality.

For a more tailored recording, you can specify details such as, "I remember having my new car, the xxxx model, delivered on my birthday. It was an extraordinary birthday, and I recall the distinct scent and texture of the leather, the exquisite color. Driving it felt effortlessly smooth, filling me with immense joy and gratitude. It was an easy and seamless process, and I continue to appreciate my car wholeheartedly."

Make it a habit to listen to this recording at least twice a day, once in the morning upon waking and again in the evening before bedtime.

Number 6: Memory/Revision Cards

Remembering cards are a handy tool consisting of a set of cards, each with blank spaces for you to fill with your desired outcomes. You can easily find these cards in most stationery shops, or you can opt for our preprinted versions.

You have the flexibility to either write out your desires on these cards or get creative with colors and pictures. You can even draw images or cut out visuals from magazines or download them from the internet to enhance the visual impact. If you're like me and drawing isn't your forte, simple matchstick men with happy faces can do the trick. Remember, the mind responds well to vibrant visuals, so feel free to use as much color as you like.

Number 7: Mirrors

Harness the incredible power of mirrors. Choose a mirror you look into every day. Your bathroom mirror is often the ideal choice, as it's where you brush your teeth and engage in daily routines. However, mirrors in hallways, dressing tables, or even in your car (as long as they don't obstruct your view) can work as well. Place a small piece of paper or a card on the mirror to remind you of what you want to remember.

Now, as you gaze into the mirror, you'll be prompted to recall your goal. Use whiteboard pens for writing on the mirror or simply write on a card or paper, cut it out, and stick it onto the mirror. It's essential to look yourself in the eyes while saying your affirmation out loud, as you remember the moment when you achieved your goal.

Maintain a positive attitude as you do this daily, and remember to infuse each day with positivity.

If you're wondering why you should adopt this practice or seeking proof of its effectiveness, consider my own experience. I've been using this technique for some time, and it works. I can briefly summarize:

My life is a good one, with lots of ease and happiness, often saying to friends, "You'll never believe this…"

I manifested my dream house, even in the most volatile housing market.

Our vacations are incredible, with smooth travel, easy parking, and delightful experiences. We fly through security, we arrive safely and happily, and we always have the loveliest holidays.

My days are filled with joy and success. While not every day is perfect, everything ultimately works out for me, my daughter, and others around me.

Remember to pay attention, practice regularly, and repeat your affirmations. Repetition is the key to mastering this technique, and remembering your future is the ultimate solution.

Remember: the point of this book is to simplify and enrich your life. I am committed to providing you with an easy, joyful journey where the results speak for themselves.

Summary – Cultivating Clarity in Desires and Intentions

1. **Emphasizing Clarity in Desires:** To harness the full potential of the Remembering Technique, it's crucial to have a clear understanding of your desires. Often, we tend to focus on what we don't want, which can lead to negativity and uncertainty. By shifting your perspective and clearly articulating and remembering what you truly want, you can bring clarity to your decisions and actions, shaping your future in every moment.

2. **The Power of Specific Asks:** To maximize the effectiveness of the Remembering Technique, it's essential to be specific and detailed when asking for what you desire. It's not enough to simply know what you don't want; you must also frame and visualize your desires in vivid detail. This precision in your desires can significantly enhance the effectiveness of the process and make it more directed and focused on achieving your goals.

3. **Transforming Complaints into Positive Requests:** Redirect the energy that might otherwise be spent on complaints or dwelling on undesired outcomes towards positive requests. Shifting your mindset in this way requires a conscious effort to focus on positive aspirations and desired outcomes.

4. **Utilizing Remembering for Desired Outcomes:** Utilize remembering techniques to strengthen your desires. When you remember the outcomes you want to achieve, you are programming your subconscious mind to actively work towards making them a reality. These remembering exercises can be as straightforward or intricate as necessary, as long as they resonate with you and align with your goals.

5. **The Simplicity and Complexity of Desires:** While the act of asking for what you want may seem simple, its implementation can be complex due to our deeply rooted habits and thought patterns. It's crucial to acknowledge this complexity and exercise patience with yourself as you transition your focus from negativity to positivity.

6. **Making Decisions Aligned with Desires:** Remembering your desires has a profound impact on your daily choices. Clarity about your goals naturally guides your decisions, bringing them into alignment with your aspirations and facilitating their manifestation in your life.

7. **The Ease of Achieving Desires:** Choose to approach your desires with the belief that their achievement can be effortless and enjoyable. This perspective not only enhances the journey's quality but also eliminates unnecessary obstacles that often stem from a mindset of struggle and difficulty.

In conclusion, Chapter 3 emphasizes the significance of having clear desires and the effectiveness of making specific requests while also highlighting the transformation of negative thought patterns into positive ones. This chapter serves as a guide for redefining the way we express our desires, underscoring the role of remembering and optimistic thinking in the pursuit of our goals and desires. It encourages readers to change their perspective and approach their goals with a mindset centered on simplicity and positivity.

Chapter Four

WHAT DO YOU WANT?

In Chapter Four, we embark on an exploratory journey to discover personalized methods of remembering.

This chapter is dedicated to uncovering the unique ways in which each of us can harness the power of remembering to shape our future. We recognize that there is no one-size-fits-all approach and delve into various techniques, from visualization to creative expression. We highlight the importance of finding a method that resonates deeply with your individual style and needs. Through this exploration, we emphasize the significance of connecting with your inner self in an enjoyable and effective manner, thereby making the practice of remembering an art form that is uniquely yours.

Goal setting

What do you want?

A car?

What type of car? A new car? An old car? A red car? A sports car?

Get specific; this is crucial. Don't settle for less; aim higher, give yourself permission to have that car. Be precise about the details, then remember that you own it. Make it tangible; visit the car, sit in it, take it for a test drive. Then return home and remember that you are now driving it. Recall how it feels, the scent, the quiet click of the door, the sense of pride as it sits on your driveway. Remember parking it, stepping out, looking back, and hearing the door lock. It's yours; remember that smile, that feeling of accomplishment. You did it, effortlessly and joyfully.

A new house?

Do you want an old house? A new one? Where do you want it? A fixer-upper to make it truly yours? A beautiful house with designer finishes, a custom-made kitchen, fully tiled bathrooms, breathtaking views from every window, tranquility, perfect parking, a double garage, an office, and a potting shed?

Now, remember how it feels to live in this house. Find a real one or draw it. Recall walking through each room, making coffee with a top-notch coffee maker, sitting on your splendid deck in the morning sun. Remember how wonderful it is to live here, how easily it came to you, as if it had been waiting for you all along.

A new job?

What is your dream job? What do you want?

Recall what brings you happiness, remember what you're passionate about, and remember that you can find a job that aligns with your passions and brings you joy.

Holidays

Dreaming of fabulous holidays? Where do you want to go? How do you want to travel? First class? By road, sea, or air? When do you want to go?

When do you want it?

Today, you might say, or even yesterday. In this new world, anything is possible. Remembering that you can have the life of your dreams is remarkably simple, especially when you've taken the time to break it down, remember exactly what you desire, and acknowledge that you can have it.

In the beginning, this process was a source of curiosity for me. I could remember some things, and they appeared almost magically, while others seemed to take a bit longer. The answer, however, is quite simple. When you remember the thing, event, or item/goal speeding its way to you, remember that it has nothing standing in its way—it's already yours. Then, simply let go and allow it to appear.

Why do you want it?

Ask yourself "Why?" once, and then ask it again, and again.

Don't underestimate the power of this simple technique. It helps you get clear and understand the emotion behind your desires. Just remember why you want it.

Write down the first "Why," and then write the second "Why." Lastly, write "Why" again. This time, really remember why. This process will ignite your passion, keep you focused, and drive you toward your goal.

The first "Why" may give you a lukewarm response, lacking emotion. The second "Why" starts to challenge your commitment to your goal. Now, remember the third "Why." You are having a conversation with yourself, your soul, your inner self. This will bring out your true reason, your deep passion for your goal, and you'll remember it easily.

Think about how you'll feel when you have it. Recall the pleasure and excitement you felt when you first learned to drive, the sense of achievement, and the freedom it gave you to get around.

Now, all you have to do is remember those same feelings as if you already have it in your future. The trick is to assume you are in the future. Your subconscious mind doesn't differentiate between real and imagined experiences. You are essentially developing a new skill, a natural habit.

While neuroscientists may not fully understand why we remember, they do know that we take in information, create neural pathways to memories, and strengthen those memories through repeated access or encoding. The more enjoyable and fun we make it, the better. Our minds thrive on fun, color, and novelty, as they break away from predictable behavior and help create lasting memories. Remember that we believe our memories, making this a powerful way to positively influence your future.

So, what do I mean by assuming to be in the future? It's quite simple. Just remember that all you need to do is assume you are in the future, looking back on your already achieved goal. Or, imagine yourself on a date after your desired event, having received your goal, and just keep remembering that.

An example scenario:

Your birthday party is set for November 30, 2023, and today's date is November 10, 2023. On November 10, 2023, you would write in your journal or diary as if you are already in the future, on December 1, 2023. You can assume, pretend, imagine, or associate yourself with that future date. Just tell yourself, "It's December 1, 2023," and remember what an incredible day it was. Write about how fantastic the entire event was, how easy it had been to organize, how all the party invitations were received, and revel in the joy of achieving it.

Remember how easy it is?

You constantly talk to yourself through your thoughts, which occur all day long. These thoughts can be good, bad, right, or wrong, and they are ongoing. On average, people have approximately 60,000 thoughts a day, and a substantial portion of them, about 75%, tend to be negative, while a significant 95% are repetitive. (This information is based on a study from 2020, as mentioned in *How Many Thoughts Do You Have Per Day? And Other FAQs (healthline.com), and insights from Dr. Fred Luskin at Stanford University.)

You have the power to shift your mindset and remember how easy it is to live in a state of flow and ease. Discover the joy of navigating life's contrasts and challenges with grace instead of getting caught up in the difficulties. It's time to break free from old patterns that yield the same results, and embrace the new you, who effortlessly moves through life with ease and grace. Always remember, the choice is yours.

And as I mentioned earlier, I live in a state of ease, flow, and happiness, and this simple adjustment has transformed my life into a positive journey where I achieve my goals, and everything falls into place effortlessly. Adding happiness to the equation is the secret sauce that changes the energy.

Never forget, you have the capability to do it.

Our brains thrive on examples and the belief that if others have achieved it, we can too. It's a shortcut to success. So, always remember that this process is easy. I've successfully done it, and countless others have as well. It's a proven method with real stories and tangible results. The stories you read here are true accounts of accomplishments that have truly happened, demonstrating the effectiveness of these techniques. Success is within your reach, and you can achieve it.

Remembering Bucket List Dreams

Dancing show win and a new car!

Not long after I started practicing my Remembering Technique, something truly extraordinary happened.

You see, there's this popular dance competition TV show on BBC called Strictly Come Dancing. Tickets for the show are incredibly hard to come by; I'd been a devoted fan since its inception in 2004 and had even entered their ticket draw several times without any luck. However, I decided I had nothing to lose, and I made a bold choice—I was going to attend the show. I remembered vividly that I had tickets and envisioned myself there, enjoying the entire experience.

After making this decision, something incredible occurred. I entered the ticket draw once more, just as I always did. But this time, within a week, I received the news that I had won tickets! I couldn't believe it—two tickets for a prerecording of the show, although there was no guarantee of actually getting inside, as they invite more people than the studio can accommodate, and you have to queue, hoping for a spot.

The initial joy of winning was followed by practical considerations. How would we get to Elstree Studios? Should we stay overnight or drive back? How long would the day be? Would the experience live up to the live Saturday night broadcasts? To be honest, I didn't really care—I had tickets. In a bold move, I decided to enter the ticket draw again, relying on the power of my Remembering Technique, and unbelievably, I won yet another set of tickets. It felt surreal.

On the day of the recording, we traveled to Elstree Studios early and joined a long queue. Excitement and nervousness coursed through me—would I actually make it inside? Would we get to be part of the experience?

The queuing turned out to be a delightful and enjoyable experience. The crowd of people waiting were lively and friendly, and the security and procedures were thorough but seamless. We met all the criteria, and to add to the excitement, we were allowed to purchase some merchandise. I couldn't resist getting the notebook, t-shirt, and bag—I had it all. While chatting with the production staff, I learned a mind-boggling fact: there were a whopping 6,000,000 entries for the tickets! Yes, 6,000,000! When I mentioned that we had won additional tickets, he couldn't believe it. I assured him it was true and looked forward to seeing him again next time.

To our amazement, we were seated in the front row on the balcony, looking down over the studio floor and stage. The magic of Harry Potter unfolded before our very eyes, creating an incredible experience. Gladys Knight graced us with her singing from a Bond movie. The dancers were not only talented but also friendly, and the entire show was nothing short of spectacular.

Despite the long day and night, time seemed to fly by. We felt incredibly fortunate—was it luck, or was it the power of the Remembering Technique?

Two weeks later, we found ourselves doing it all over again. This time, we knew to arrive earlier, and we were familiar with the procedures. To our delight, we secured front-row seats right by Dave Archer's band.

As we watched the show unfold, we were once again in awe of the amazing dancing. But this time, something truly special happened—we witnessed a TV first, a dance performed in pouring rain. It was an incredible experience to be part of Strictly Come Dancing history while also realizing my dream.

Living in a world of "you'll never believe this," I've got another incredible story to share. As my new world began to unfold, I found myself in need of a new car. I reside in a city with old roads, high curbs, and a parking situation that can only be described as a nightmare. New cars in this city tend to endure a lot of wear and tear—scratches, dents, and abuse are all too common. (By the way, I've used the Remembering Technique to always secure a parking space, so don't hesitate to apply it to that aspect of life too.)

But let's get back to my story. Given the unique challenges of city living, I decided that I wanted a new car—one that could handle the tough terrain yet still make the school run enjoyable. My choice? A Volkswagen EOS. But I didn't want just any car; I wanted a convertible with specific features: cream leather interior, all the bells and whistles, a touch screen command system for the stereo, satellite navigation, automatic transmission...you get the idea. I'm starting to sound like a car advertisement, aren't I?

Well, let's move on from the car details. I began to remember that I already had the car of my dreams. It was fast, sleek, and absolutely perfect. I loved driving it with the roof up and the sunroof open, or with the roof down, enjoying the incredible sound system. I could listen to my audiobooks in stereo or sing along to fun songs while heading to the coast.

As I continued to remember, my vision of driving this beautiful convertible hardtop car became clearer and more vivid with each passing day. And then, it happened. The car I had envisioned materialized—it was the right price, the perfect color, and had the exact interior I had remembered. What's even more incredible is that it was located just down the road from the Elstree Studios. I had the opportunity to go see it, think it over, attend the show, and, if I liked it, return for a second visit to buy it and drive it away. And you know what? That's exactly what I did.

Summary – Exploring Diverse Techniques of Remembering

1. **Embracing Different Approaches:** The journey of remembering involves exploring various personal methods. Whether through words, imagery, or creative techniques, finding your unique path is essential. Remember, memorizing your future can be tailored to your individual style and preference.

2. **Utilizing the Power of Visualization:** Visualization is a potent tool in the art of remembering. It involves vividly picturing your goals and aspirations in your mind's eye. You can use various mediums like mental images, written words, or physical representations. Immerse yourself in the future, remembering it as already accomplished.

3. **Connecting with Your Inner Self:** Building a connection with your inner child or the playful aspect of yourself can lead to remarkable outcomes. By collaborating with your inner being, higher self, or subconscious mind, you unlock a realm of potential. The essential element is to establish a connection, have conversations, and engage with this facet of your existence in a manner that feels effortless and delightful.

4. **Practice and Persistence:** As with any skill, mastering the art of remembering demands practice. It's akin to learning how to walk or ride a bicycle—it necessitates

time and persistent effort. Nonetheless, you can expedite this learning curve. When you wholeheartedly and consistently embrace the technique, you'll experience swifter and more profound results.

5. **Customizing the Remembering Experience:** The beauty of remembering lies in its flexibility. You may discover that memory cards, mirrors, journals, or diaries suit you best. Every approach offers distinct advantages, and you can explore them to identify your ideal fit. It involves capitalizing on your strengths and inclinations.

6. **The Role of Creativity and Fun:** Infusing the process with creativity and enjoyment is crucial. When engaging with your memories, allowing your imaginative and playful side to thrive can yield delightful outcomes. It's not merely about monotonous repetition but about injecting joy and creativity into the journey.

7. **Expanding Your Techniques Over Time:** As you grow more comfortable with the process of remembering, broaden and fine-tune your techniques. Modify and advance your methods as you gain a deeper understanding of what resonates with you. The path of remembering is ever-changing, and your approach can evolve in sync with your personal development.

In conclusion, Chapter 4 brings together practical advice on exploring a range of remembering techniques with insights into the significance of personalization, creativity, and inner self connection. This chapter acts as an empowering guide to discovering and enhancing your distinct method of remembering, underlining the importance of consistent practice, persistence, and enjoyment in mastering this transformative skill.

Chapter Five

WHERE AND WHEN

Chapter Five delves into the pivotal role of repetition and persistence in mastering the art of remembering. This chapter emphasizes the paramount significance of consistent practice in etching our desired visions and thoughts indelibly into the fabric of our minds.

Within these pages, we explore how the discipline of regular remembering not only ingrains our aspirations deeply but also transforms these aspirations into tangible realities. The crux of the matter lies in understanding that, although the concept may appear straightforward, sustaining this practice can be a profound journey unto itself, necessitating unwavering dedication, patience, and a clear understanding of our "why." Through this chapter, we unravel the intrinsic potency of repetition, recognizing it not merely as a tool for reinforcement but as a formidable catalyst for enduring change and achievement.

Where and when do I practice remembering?

The choice is yours. Personally, I am a morning person, so I find my best practice in the morning. However, you may be more productive in the evening. It's essential to align your practice with your natural rhythm.

I prefer to write at my kitchen table, but remember that your practice space can be anywhere that provides quiet and focus. This could be a quiet room, your car, or any location where distractions are minimal. The key is to create an environment where your mind can flow freely.

Once you've established your quiet space and time, you might want to accelerate your practice. One effective way to do this is by:

Meditation

Remember, you matter. It's crucial to make time for moments of quiet reflection as it significantly contributes to your overall well-being. Allowing yourself to simply be, without any specific agenda, has been proven to be effective. There are various meditation techniques you can explore to find what resonates best with you. Personally, I find guided meditations to be the most effective for me. They help me enter a state of silence and connection with my inner self by quieting the constant chatter in my mind. You can remember to prioritize relaxation, stay open to deeper connections within yourself, and find joy in these moments of stillness and self-discovery.

Remember to pause and make time for yourself. This simple practice can lead to a calmer and happier life. It's a way to ensure that you're being the best version of yourself.

If you want to incorporate this technique throughout your day, consider setting alarms on your phone or other timekeeping devices. For example, you can set an alarm to go off every hour, and when it does, take a moment to remember:

- Today is a good day.
- I am achieving so much so easily and happily.
- I remember I felt so good.
- I remember my daughter had a great day.
- I remember … whatever is relevant for you.

Please visit my website for a free guided meditation; you will find it under tools and resources. (www.TheRememberingTechnique.com)

Author's Note

As you can see, transitioning from past remembering to future remembering is a seamless process that can make manifesting your desires feel effortless.

You're essentially utilizing a skill set that you already possess and redirecting it to work in a more beneficial way for you.

Think about how easy it is to remember a beautiful summer day on the beach, with the sun warming your soul, the sound of the sea, the singing birds, and that overall sense of happiness, relaxation, and peace. You feel perfect. Now, take all those positive feelings and remember that you have them today. You become the sunshine, the calm, and the magic in your present moment. Remember that you possess these qualities right now, and today is a great day.

Summary – The Power of Repetition and Persistence in Remembering

1. **Understanding the Importance of Repetition:** Repetition serves as the foundation upon which the art of remembering can stand. Although it may appear straightforward, maintaining a consistent practice of this technique can sometimes pose a challenge. Nonetheless, the benefits of this discipline are vast, as it firmly embeds your desired thoughts and visions into your subconscious mind.

2. **Consistency in Practice:** Regular practice is the key to harnessing the power of remembering. Although it may seem like the simplest task, there will be moments when it feels especially daunting. However, keep in mind that the strength of your "Why" can make this process feel effortless. When your motivation is sufficiently compelling, this practice seamlessly integrates into your daily life.

3. **Applying Repetition to Daily Life:** Employ repetition to reinforce positive thoughts and memories in every facet of your life. Whether you are recalling success in your personal or professional pursuits or reshaping your mindset, consistent practice of positive remembering bolsters these neural connections, enhancing their effectiveness.

4. **Expanding the Power of Memory Beyond the Self:**
   While repetition is frequently centered on personal
   objectives and aspirations, it can also be utilized to
   positively impact others. Consistently recalling success,
   happiness, and well-being for those in your life can
   contribute to a positive transformation in their lives too.

5. **Challenges in Maintaining Practice:** Recognize
   that maintaining a consistent practice isn't always
   straightforward. Life's distractions and challenges
   can sometimes hinder your ability to focus on your
   remembering practice. During these moments, remind
   yourself of the transformative power of this technique
   and recommit to your practice.

6. **The Role of Discipline in Remembering:** Discipline
   plays a crucial role in this practice. It involves making
   a commitment to yourself and maintaining it, even
   when faced with challenges. The discipline applied
   to remembering isn't just about achieving particular
   goals but also about fostering a mindset of success and
   positivity that extends to all aspects of your life.

In conclusion, Chapter 5 underscores the significance of
repetition and consistency in the practice of remembering,
highlighting how this discipline can profoundly influence
personal growth and goal achievement. This chapter serves
as a motivational guide, emphasizing the transformative
effects of maintaining a regular practice of remembering on
both personal aspirations and the well-being of others.

Chapter Six

TIME: HOW FAR IN ADVANCE, AND TIME DISTORTION

Chapter Six opens the door to the profound possibilities of using the art of remembering to mold our perception of time and future occurrences. It introduces the concept of visualizing events before their actual realization and explores the ways in which this technique can influence our experiences and outcomes.

This chapter provides practical insights into applying this method in various life scenarios, from preparing for significant life events to altering our perception of time in everyday situations. This chapter will unravel the intricate relationship between memory, time, and intention, demonstrating how the power of remembering can not only help us foresee and shape the future but also redefine our connection with time itself.

How much time in advance do you need to remember?

What a great question. Choosing the right technique for you depends on your goals and preferences. When I first began using this method, I decided to apply it to planning a holiday.

Here's what I did:

I wrote down the details of our holiday trip in a diary, including the destination (Italy), the travelers (myself, my daughter, and my nephew), the arrangements (flights, car rental, self-catering villa), the activities (beach, exploring), the journey there and back, and the overall experience.

I assumed that it was already the 30th of July 2018 (even though I wrote it on the 5th of July for a holiday planned from the 15th to the 25th of July 2018).

I vividly remembered in my diary how we efficiently packed our suitcases with the perfect outfits for the trip, making it seem effortless and effective. The car ride to the airport was remarkably smooth, as we experienced a state of flow and ease. Filled with happiness and excitement, we drove calmly and serenely, with no traffic on the road, ensuring a clear run to the airport. Once there, parking was a breeze, and we seamlessly navigated through the airport with ease and effortlessness. The security clearance process was swift, and everything just flowed seamlessly.

There were no issues, and our meal at the airport was a delightful experience. Finding a table was no trouble at all, and the food arrived quickly, adding an element of fun to our relaxed and calm state. Our flight was on time, and we happily boarded at the front of the queue, even indulging in a cheeky visit to WHSmith to grab some comics and magazines for the flight.

The flight itself was nothing short of amazing, with an exceptional crew that made the journey all the more enjoyable. The flight arrived early and safely, and we breezed through passport control without any delays. The memory of that experience remains vivid. I envisioned that, to our pleasant surprise, we were first in line at the car hire desk, and the kind attendant noticed that I was traveling alone with two children. His generosity shone through as he offered a free car upgrade, brightening my day. Leaving the airport in our fantastic, upgraded hire car, we drove effortlessly to the supermarket, giggling with joy at the feasts we were going to have. Loading the car was a breeze, filled with happiness and ease, and we embarked on our journey to the house. Time seemed to fly by. One moment we were leaving the car park, and the next, we were turning off at our designated junction.

The house was immaculate, welcoming us with its cleanliness and readiness to provide a fantastic holiday experience. It didn't take us long to unload the car and settle in, and the happiness we all felt was palpable.

Throughout our holiday, we were blessed with amazing weather, perfectly suited to our fair skin. Our days out were wonderfully planned and executed, making it an unforgettable trip. The memories of that easy, enjoyable holiday stay with us fondly.

As our wonderful vacation came to an end, we seamlessly went about cleaning the house and handling the linens. Packing up and loading the car was just as effortless as our journey out. Returning to the airport was a breeze, and returning the rental car was just as easy as picking it up.

Clearing security at the airport was as smooth as a warm knife through butter, and our dinner was a sublime experience. Passport control posed no challenge, and our flight was punctual and uneventful. Upon landing, we navigated passport control once more, picked up some groceries at M&S, and made our way to our car with ease. Once again, the motorway was clear, allowing us to drive effortlessly while feeling happy, light, and immensely grateful for our wonderful and memorable holiday.

How lucky are we to have had such a wonderful time? I remember it so well. Who could forget?

Short version:

I remember how everything fell into place effortlessly during our trip. Packing was a breeze, the journey flowed smoothly, and our happiness was palpable. We parked easily, breezed through security, and boarded our flight with such ease. We secured seats promptly, and the flight itself was calm and safe. The holiday was truly amazing, characterized by ease, serenity, and boundless happiness.

Our return journey surpassed even the ease of our outbound trip. Closing up the house was effortless, and the trip back was filled with joy, ease, and an abundance of happy moments. I remember it vividly, marked by its sheer effortlessness and happiness.

Next, I decided to challenge myself by remembering a typical working day. Could I recall it with the same level of detail?

This is what I wrote:

> Wednesday 6.12.18 (written at 6:00 a.m. on 6.12.18)
>
> What a great day it was! I felt calm, serene, and confident. Everything worked out perfectly for me and even exceeded my expectations. Today was truly amazing.
>
> I looked amazing, and it required no effort at all. I arrived at work early, and everything flowed smoothly.
>
> I remember the day so vividly and clearly. It was a remarkable day where I accomplished

everything I needed and more. I made decisions that were not only beneficial for me but also for the business. What a fantastic day! I absolutely loved it. Today was truly exceptional.

Another version may go like this:

Wednesday 6.12.18 (written at 6:00 a.m. on 6.12.18)

I remember when I chose to have a great day, and everything just flowed effortlessly. Money, happiness, calmness, and success seemed to come my way naturally. I felt incredibly happy and content.

On that remarkable day, I achieved several incredible things:

1. I had excellent and joyful sales, with lovely customers and a constant flow of happy money.
2. All the paperwork I needed to complete was effortlessly and happily taken care of.
3. My problems seemed to simply melt away.
4. I distinctly recall that solutions to any challenges either appeared before I realized there was a problem or, if a problem did arise, it was swiftly and joyfully resolved. Everything just flowed perfectly for me.

—⟞⟞⟞—

A quick story about something that happened during my day:

I encountered a challenging situation with a customer who had lost a diamond from her ring. Although it was not my fault, as she had purchased the ring two years prior, I empathized with her. People often misunderstand how jewelry works, and diamonds can sometimes break or fall out without causing any damage to the ring. Despite the circumstances, I remained as supportive as possible. In her eyes, I had sold her a faulty ring, and she was now finding fault with every aspect of it, even though she had cherished it for years and wore it daily. To maintain goodwill, I offered to assist her with the issue.

I presented her with several possible solutions, and she took some time to consider them. Later, when she had returned home and I had continued my work, I received a call from her. I answered the call, uncertain about how we would resolve the issue. To my surprise, she had a proposal of her own. I found her proposal acceptable, and I was relieved to see the problem resolved. It was a win-win situation, and I was grateful that the issue was resolved to both our satisfaction.

Don't forget, I remembered that I had the solution/answer to my problems.

1. I just loved the day, just loved it!
2. What a great day. It was exactly that…and more!

At the end of the day, take a moment to reflect and tick off all the things you accomplished so easily and joyfully. You'll be amazed at what you can achieve through this practice.

When I remember these future events with all the details as easy, flowing, and happy experiences that I desire, I make sure to document them in a diary or a journal, complete with the date. However, you can also choose to do this without specifying a date, allowing these manifestations to unfold in their own time.

Once I've successfully achieved the desired goal/outcome/ solution, I sign it and include the date I initially wrote it at the bottom. This helps me recognize that I remembered and documented it on that particular date when I review my journal in real life, reinforcing its effectiveness.

Time Distortion:

Time Distortion is one of my favorite techniques, and it can be applied quickly with remarkable results. Here is a true story of how this works for me:

My daughter was having a few extra ski lessons before her school ski trip.

The dry ski slope was typically a 35-minute drive away under normal traffic conditions. However, the only available ski lessons for my daughter were scheduled on a Friday evening during rush hour traffic. The satellite navigation estimated the travel time to be over an hour, and this didn't account for any unforeseen accidents or delays. Despite my efforts to remember and visualize a safe and timely journey, the reality of heavy traffic during the holiday season posed a challenge. It was two weeks before Christmas, and the roads were congested and gridlocked with a seemingly endless stream of vehicles. All I could think about was making it to my daughter's ski lesson at 6 p.m.

It was now 4:45 p.m., and I should have collected her at 4:20 p.m. I needed to do some extra work that couldn't wait. I remembered I collected her easily and safely. We set out, all was good, and I was calm. I just kept remembering how easy it was for me to get through the traffic.

Sure enough, we encountered every possible delay—the people pushing in, the people driving really slow. It's like a test of your patience, and I love the way the universe tests your resolve. It was okay, as I knew we would get there in time, with time to spare. My daughter, however, as a teenager, has yet to learn this. "The chap in front can't drive properly," she muttered. "Why is there so much traffic?"

Her questions and judgments were abundant, but I remained calm, knowing we would arrive on time and that everything would be fine. While driving, I remembered that the driver in front of us needed to get out of the way. As we approached the roundabout, I noticed he was going in the same direction. However, as I entered the roundabout and encountered the traffic jam, I suddenly saw a gap to my left. I maneuvered into it, and we smoothly transitioned out of the traffic jam and into the flow of traffic. The man in front was no longer an issue, and my daughter complimented my driving, saying, "Good job, Mum." It felt completely natural and easy, as if I was being guided.

We then encountered another traffic jam on the motorway. While sitting there, I began to remember that the cars in front of us needed to move out of the way. Miraculously, they did just that. The traffic started to shift into the next lane, creating more room for us to continue on our journey and arrive on time. As I checked the estimated time of arrival, it showed 6 p.m., right on schedule.

The ski lesson was scheduled for 6 p.m., and we were supposed to arrive at 5:55 p.m. I realized that this was cutting it a bit too close to the lesson time, as my daughter needed some time to put on her skis and get on the slope. But I decided to turn it into a game, as I enjoy playing games. So, I began to remember that the clock said 5:45 p.m. As if responding to my playful game, the estimated time of arrival then miraculously shifted to 5:50 p.m. It seemed like the universe was having some fun with me.

I remembered it as 5:45 p.m., and despite various challenges like traffic clearing, taking the wrong turn, and encountering a closed road, I stayed committed to my memory of arriving at 5:45 p.m. Remarkably, we indeed arrived at 5:45 p.m. I dropped my daughter at the front door and enjoyed a wonderful evening of skiing and après-ski at the venue.

On the way back, I couldn't resist a little challenge. The navigation indicated that we would arrive home by 8:20 p.m., but I decided I wanted to be home at 8:10 p.m. It was just a playful experiment.

The universe had another surprise in store for me. I was cruising along in the outside lane, and in front of me was a big, shiny lorry adorned with numerous red lights, much like the Coca-Cola Christmas lorry.

Directly behind the lorry was a small car. As I continued my journey and enjoyed the sight of the lorry, the unexpected happened. The small car behind the lorry suddenly braked and swiftly pulled into my lane, right where I was. Fortunately, I had enough time to react and swerve, avoiding a collision with the oncoming vehicle. My daughter remarked, "Nice driving," and added, "That was a close one." However, I didn't feel the same intensity. Yes, it was a close call, but I remained calm throughout the ordeal, just as I had remembered. As expected, the journey unfolded seamlessly, within the speed limit and without any further incidents.

We arrived home at 8:10 p.m., feeling joyful, content, and safe.

Another way to use this technique is when a day or event seems to be dragging on slowly. Instead of constantly checking the clock, simply remember the time you would like it to be, and only check when it's that time.

Conversely, if you want to make a day feel longer and savor each moment, remember a time when it felt like it was going slower and you were thoroughly enjoying it. By remembering that feeling, you can make the current day feel more extended and enjoyable, effectively slowing down time in your perception.

Summary – Mastering Time and Remembering Future Events

1. **Understanding Time and Remembering:** Remembering for future events is a powerful tool that can influence how we experience and manage time. Whether you're recalling a past successful holiday trip or preparing for an upcoming event, the timing of your remembering can have a profound effect on its outcomes.

2. **Practical Application in Everyday Life:** An illustrative example of this concept is holiday preparation. By positively remembering each phase of the journey, from packing to the travel experience, you establish a foundation for the actual experience to unfold harmoniously. This technique is applicable to various future events, including exams and significant meetings.

3. **Time Distortion through Remembering:** The practice of remembering can also serve as a tool to manipulate our perception of time. For instance, in situations where you find yourself running behind schedule for an appointment, engaging in the act of remembering yourself arriving punctually can, with practice, result in a remarkable alteration of how events unfold. This seemingly magical ability to bend time in your favor does require consistent practice to master.

4. **Transforming Old Memories into New:** Each of us holds memories that may evoke unfavorable emotions. However, through the deliberate act of remembering these memories from a different perspective, we possess the power to transform our emotional responses. This practice doesn't negate the events that occurred but rather reshapes our emotional reactions, effectively neutralizing negative sentiments and replacing them with more positive or neutral ones.

5. **Remembering for Short- and Long-Term Goals:** Regardless of whether you're recalling recent accomplishments or visualizing long-term aspirations, the art of remembering serves as a pivotal practice. It entails vividly remembering yourself achieving your objectives and immersing yourself in the emotions linked to that triumph.

6. **Harnessing Memory for Personal Growth:** Remembering extends beyond the realm of reminiscing about past events; it also encompasses the ability to project positive outcomes into the future. This capacity serves as a potent tool for personal growth, enabling you to reshape your future by modifying the way you remember and envision forthcoming events.

7. **Incorporating Repetition for Effectiveness:** Just like any skill, the effectiveness of remembering enhances with practice. Consistently recalling positive outcomes for both near-term and long-term future

events strengthens your desired path and makes the attainment of your goals more achievable.

In conclusion, Chapter 6 integrates practical strategies for utilizing the art of remembering to shape future events, along with insights into how this technique can impact our perception of time and emotional reactions to past experiences. This chapter serves as a comprehensive guide to harnessing the power of remembering and memory to foster personal growth, attain goals, and cultivate a more positive perspective on life's journey.

Chapter Seven

THE SCIENCE

In Chapter Seven, we journey into the fascinating realm of the science behind remembering.

This chapter sheds light on the intricate processes that underlie our ability to remember and envision the future, seamlessly blending ancient mnemonic techniques with contemporary neurological insights. Here, we explore the biological foundations of memory, delving into the mechanisms by which our brains encode, store, and retrieve information.

This exploration is not merely theoretical; it provides a foundational understanding that equips us to wield the art of remembering more effectively in our daily lives. By bridging the gap between science and practical application, this chapter offers a profound appreciation for the power of remembering and its potential to reshape our perceptions and experiences.

Interesting Facts and Science

Another technique that has endured through the ages is the Greek concept of a "Memory Palace." This method of memorization revolves around constructing a visual narrative around the words or characters one wishes to remember. Even today, this technique finds application in the practices of exceptional memorizers, such as those who memorize thousands of digits of Pi. I have a friend who held the title of world champion in this endeavor; he was quite the hit at Christmas parties and even had the opportunity to appear on The Oprah Winfrey Show.

It's essential to note that Pi is an infinite number. My friend held a Guinness® record for reciting Pi up to 22,500 digits, showcasing the remarkable power of remembering. The current record stands at an astonishing 70,000 digits. These memory champions, including my friend, are not fundamentally different from us; they have simply mastered the required techniques. Initially, my friend embarked on this journey to improve his exam performance and secure a promotion, and his dedication eventually led to his remarkable record.

Creating a Memory Palace is a simple technique. You envision walking through a familiar location you know well, and then you add unusual associations or objects that relate to what you want to remember. For example, you might imagine a frog wearing a tuxedo sitting on your kitchen counter.

This technique can help you remember various details. For example, if you're reading a book and want to remember that the butler died (croaked) in the kitchen, you could associate it with the image of the frog in the tuxedo on your kitchen counter. The key is to create memorable and sometimes bizarre associations that stick in your mind.

Professional memorizers often emphasize the importance of making the elements within your Memory Palace as outrageous, bizarre, humorous, or even raunchy as possible. These extraordinary and sometimes absurd associations are more likely to stick in your memory and be unforgettable.

All of these techniques are interconnected with the fundamental understanding of how memory functions.

How Memories Are Encoded into the Brain

Encoding memories into the brain is indeed a biological process rooted in sensory experiences. Our brains tend to remember events and information more vividly when they are associated with strong sensory inputs and emotional experiences. These sensory and emotional cues play a significant role in encoding and subsequently recalling memories.

These sensory experiences alone do not constitute a memory, but because of their significance, your brain encodes them into a lasting memory.

This process occurs primarily in the hippocampus and the frontal cortex of your brain, working in tandem. These two regions are thought to be responsible for analyzing the events you experience and determining whether they should be stored as long-term memories. It's the process that transforms short-term memories into long-term ones.

While we understand that different aspects of an event are stored in various parts of the brain, the exact mechanism of how these elements are integrated during memory recall is still a subject of ongoing research for neuroscientists.

Memories are fundamentally stored as electrical and chemical signals in the brain. Nerve cells form connections in specific patterns known as synapses, and the process of remembering involves your brain activating these synapses.

Building a memory is akin to instructing your brain's electrician to install new wiring. When you remember something, it's like flipping the light switch, and you witness the wiring function as intended—the light comes on.

New research indicates that this brain wiring isn't fixed, but instead undergoes constant changes. The brain cells collaborate to optimize efficiency, sometimes relocating certain memory pathways while preserving them, and in other instances, cutting off specific electrical pathways altogether. This adaptability offers the potential for deliberate change and improvement.

As synapses in the brain continue to fire, they become stronger as the brain allocates more resources to ensure their stability. This ongoing adaptability and transformation within the brain are known as neuroplasticity. It's widely recognized that neurons that wire together tend to fire together, illustrating how this principle can be harnessed to attain your desired goals and aspirations.

This demonstrates the effectiveness of repetition and the power of reshaping your memories. It's important to keep in mind that the brain cannot distinguish between real and imagined experiences. Use this to create/imagine anything you want, to make it your reality.

Summary – The Science Behind Remembering

1. **The Ancient Art of Memory:** The "Memory Palace," an ancient Greek technique, plays a pivotal role in the art of memorization. It involves constructing vivid visual narratives around the concepts or items you wish to remember. By infusing these recollections with bizarre, humorous, or unconventional imagery, you significantly enhance their memorability. This approach underscores the power of creative recall, a method still favored by modern memory champions.

2. **The Biological Basis of Memory:** Understanding how memories are encoded in the brain unveils the intriguing nexus between biology and psychology. Memories originate from sensory experiences and find their encoding within the hippocampus and frontal cortex. These cerebral regions analyze and determine which short-term memories transition into enduring ones. This biological process unites disparate experiences stored across various brain regions during the process of recall.

3. **Electrical and Chemical Nature of Memories:** Fundamentally, memories consist of electrical and chemical signals within the brain. Neurons form intricate patterns of connections called synapses, and the act of remembering involves activating these synaptic

pathways. Constructing a memory parallels the process of wiring in the brain, while recalling it resembles turning on a light switch to illuminate a room.

4. **Neuroplasticity and Memory:** Contemporary research underscores the brain's adaptability, a phenomenon referred to as neuroplasticity. This dynamic quality means that the pathways associated with memories can be reconfigured, either strengthening or weakening their influence. Neuroplasticity serves as the underlying principle behind practices like remembering and visualization, empowering us to reframe our experiences and perspectives.

5. **Repetition and Reinforcement in Memory:** The act of remembering enhances and fortifies these synaptic connections, rendering them more efficient with repeated use. This underscores the significance of repetition in memory training, as it reinforces these neural pathways, leading to easier and more resilient recall.

6. **Applying Memory Techniques to Life:** Just as memory athletes employ techniques to memorize extensive data, we can utilize similar methods to enrich our everyday experiences. Whether it's retaining crucial information, acquiring new skills, or reshaping our perspectives, the practice of remembering serves as a potent instrument for personal growth and accomplishment.

In conclusion, Chapter 7 integrates ancient memory techniques and contemporary scientific insights to offer a comprehensive exploration of the mechanics of remembering. This chapter serves as an enlightening resource on the biological and psychological foundations of memory, illustrating how these principles can be harnessed to improve memory, reshape perceptions, and facilitate personal growth.

Chapter Eight

BLOCKS

Chapter Eight delves into the crucial aspect of overcoming obstacles through the practice of remembering. It explores transformative strategies that help us approach life's challenges with resilience and positivity.

By harnessing the power of altering our perceptions and memories related to past, present, and future hurdles, we can turn obstacles into opportunities for personal growth and success.

This chapter guides us in embracing change, shedding limiting beliefs, and utilizing positive visualization to navigate difficulties, ultimately empowering us to conquer any challenges that life may throw our way.

Getting Out of Your Own Way

To achieve what you desire, you must be willing to embrace change. Change is a constant part of life, and nothing remains static. You have the ability to remember how to embody various qualities, such as confidence, effective public speaking, self-kindness, happiness, self-love, and popularity among your peers. You can remember how to attain financial freedom and maintain good health. Remembering is the initial step, and as you open yourself to new possibilities, behaviors, and approaches, remind yourself that it can be effortless.

Let go of the old belief that success has to be hard work.

While you remember and manifest your desires, you might encounter persistent challenges. Always remember to release any blocks or limiting beliefs. This process may require repeated efforts, but it's valuable. Keep remembering the new version of yourself, the one that finds it effortless, drawing from your years of remembering. Now, focus on remembering your future.

As the technique unfolds, you may find you get certain results you didn't expect.

You'll start to perceive things differently. Remember to clear any remaining blocks from your past, present, and future. Know that it's already accomplished.

Summary – Overcoming Obstacles through Remembering

1. **Embracing Change and Understanding Obstacles:** Recognize that change is an inherent aspect of life and embracing it is essential for personal development. It's important to acknowledge that obstacles and challenges are a natural part of the human experience. However, it's our response to these challenges that ultimately determines the course of our journey. Transforming our approach to obstacles requires actively reimagining our potential and capabilities.

2. **The Role of Positivity in Facing Challenges:** While confronting obstacles, maintaining a positive mindset is crucial. Negative thinking can become a self-perpetuating cycle, making it challenging to break free. However, consciously aligning with positivity can elevate your mental and emotional state. This shift to a higher vibration opens up new possibilities and transforms the process of overcoming obstacles into a path of personal growth.

3. **Changing Your Inner Narrative:** Often, we find ourselves trapped in negative thought patterns, especially when dealing with challenges. To break free from these patterns, redirect your focus towards positive aspects and let this shift redefine your reality. Simple affirmations, such as "Today is a great day," can serve as

powerful intentions and reshape your perspective on the obstacles you encounter.

4. **Finding Lightness and Joy in Life:** Life shouldn't always be taken with utmost seriousness. Incorporating fun, lightness, and humor into your experiences can profoundly impact how you tackle challenges. Liberating yourself from the shackles of worry and negativity empowers you to confront obstacles with a more balanced and optimistic perspective.

5. **Transforming Past Memories and Experiences:** Negative past experiences have the potential to shape our perception and response to current challenges. However, opting to remember these events differently by emphasizing positive outcomes or neutralizing negative emotions can be transformative. This process not only helps in releasing old, unhelpful emotions, but also contributes to a healing journey.

6. **Practicing Consistency and Repetition:** Like any skill, maintaining a consistent practice of positive remembering and memory transformation can be challenging but rewarding. Maintaining strong motivation to integrate these techniques into your life can simplify the process, ensuring they become an integral part of your daily routine.

7. **Empowering Yourself and Others in Overcoming Challenges:** Your journey of positivity and transformation extends beyond personal benefit; it

positively influences those around you, contributing to a more joyful and harmonious environment. By adopting a positive mindset and transforming your experiences, you become a beacon of inspiration for others to follow.

In conclusion, Chapter 8 provides strategies for cultivating a positive mindset, transforming negative experiences, and emphasizing the significance of self-forgiveness and regular practice. It underscores the importance of embracing positivity, releasing negativity, and harnessing the power of remembering to enhance personal well-being and create a positive impact on the world, particularly in the face of life's challenges.

Chapter Nine

HEALTH

Chapter Nine explores the art of surmounting obstacles, a pivotal skill for personal growth and success.

This chapter delves into the impact of embracing change and breaking free from mental barriers on our life's journey.

By combining personal insights with practical strategies, it will guide us as we navigate the unexpected challenges that life presents. It emphasizes shifting our perspective from resistance to acceptance and from limitation to possibility.

By mastering the ability to transform obstacles into stepping stones, we unlock a world of opportunities and experiences, illustrating how inner transformations can manifest as significant external changes.

Remember perfect health in every way, with every cell of your body radiating well-being. Remember nourishing your body with the right foods, feeling amazing, and appreciating your physical self. Remember your strong constitution. Above all, remember that you are profoundly happy, exceptionally healthy, and incredibly wise.

Remembering Healing

Healing/Helping

CantheRemembering Technique help to heal? It certainly can!

Here is a true story about a six-year-old girl. She had a wonderful day out with her grandmother, making cherished memories. However, upon returning to her parents' care, she suddenly fell seriously ill and began having seizures. Typically, seizures are brief, lasting only seconds or minutes, but this time was different. The little girl had seizures for hours, and her condition rapidly worsened, requiring an urgent trip to the hospital. Her health was in jeopardy.

The entire family rushed to the hospital, but due to the severity of the child's condition, only the parents were permitted to stay by her side. The grandmother, filled with anxiety, felt helpless and didn't know how to assist. In her desperation, she made a phone call at 4:00 a.m., seeking guidance on what steps to take.

She was then told to place her hands on the child and focus on remembering the image of the child being healthy and happily riding her bike, just as she had been earlier that day.

She continued to remember the child as healthy, joyful, and riding her bike, with the belief that this is how the child would appear the following day.

With only the parents permitted to see the child, the grandmother relayed the instructions to her daughter-in-law, who followed them diligently. She placed her hands on the child and focused on remembering the child as healthy and happy, just as she had been that day.

Not long after she started to remember the little girl as she was that day, seeing her quite clearly well and happy, the little girl made a full recovery without any lasting effects, which brought immense relief and joy to everyone.

Following my ski holiday with the children, I encountered a knee problem that required an ACL reconstruction. The surgery was scheduled, and in retrospect, I began to remember how smoothly the operation went, the exceptional support I received, and the surprisingly swift healing of my leg. I could vividly recall the speedy recovery process, with the operation proceeding seamlessly, a swift discharge from the hospital, and my leg healing in record time.

During my physiotherapy sessions, my therapists were astonished by the exceptional range of movement and strength I had regained in my knee. I vividly recalled feeling profound gratitude for the newfound flexibility and the absence of pain in my knee.

I was discharged from physiotherapy a full six weeks ahead of schedule. It was truly an outstanding outcome.

Summary – The Power of Remembering in Healing and Health

1. **Remembering Perfect Health:** Remembering can serve as a powerful tool in the maintenance and restoration of our health. Through regular visualization of ourselves in a state of perfect health, cultivating an appreciation for our bodies, and affirming our overall well-being, we wield the ability to influence our physical condition. Phrases such as "I remember I choose foods that are right for me" and "I remember I am joyful, healthy, and wise" act as daily affirmations, further strengthening our dedication to our health.

2. **The Story of Healing:** This chapter shares a real-life account of a young girl who faced a health crisis. In this pivotal moment, her family turned to the Remembering Technique to envision her recovery. They concentrated on visualizing her as happy, healthy, and participating in everyday activities, such as riding her bike. This collective act of remembering played a vital role in the girl's recuperation, highlighting the potential of remembering in the healing journey.

3. **Personal Experience with Post-Operative Recovery:** Drawing from personal experience, this chapter illustrates the significant role of remembering in post-operative recovery. By recalling a successful operation and a swift healing process, this chapter

highlights how such remembering can contribute to remarkable physical recovery. The early discharge from physiotherapy serves as a testament to the mind's power in influencing the body's healing journey.

4. **Harnessing Remembering for Physical Well-being:** This chapter underscores the crucial role of the Remembering Technique in preserving and enhancing our physical well-being. It provides readers with practical guidance on utilizing this technique to visualize and attain a state of perfect health, showcasing its practicality through real-life examples.

In conclusion, Chapter Nine integrates personal anecdotes and actionable techniques to highlight the significant role of remembering in the context of health and recovery. By illustrating how deliberate visualization and positive affirmations can impact our physical well-being, this chapter underscores the mind-body connection and the potency of thought in shaping our health journey.

Chapter Ten

WEALTH

Chapter Ten ventures into the realm of creating financial abundance through the Remembering Technique. This chapter explores the concept of wealth as an energy and how to manifest it in our lives through remembering and mental reinforcement. It provides practical exercises to shift our mindset from scarcity to abundance.

By using positive remembering and surrounding ourselves with symbols of prosperity, we can attract financial success and transform our relationship with money. It's a journey towards realizing that wealth is not just a physical entity but an achievable state of mind.

Financial Results

The only thing standing in the way of financial success is you. So, how can you remove those self-imposed barriers?

Start by acknowledging that wealth is an energy and that it's infinite. It's already within you. How can you turn this energy into real cash?

Try this: Get a large denomination bill, a $50 or $100 bill. If you don't have the physical note, you can try with fake notes. I often bought packets of these from gift shops, Amazon, or fun/joke shops. Just make sure to get the largest denomination available.

After placing the entire packet in your pocket, take yourself on a pretend shopping spree, firmly remembering that you possess the financial means to purchase anything that catches your eye. Visualize yourself buying a $500 jacket or a $1,000 sofa, maintaining the mental image that you have the money (even if it's just the fake notes) readily available in your pocket.

I also keep copies of $50 notes or chocolate bars printed to look like $50 notes in different spots, like the kitchen cupboards or the bedroom. This helps me remember that I have these notes in my purse. I make sure to place them everywhere—at home, in my car, and in the office—so that I'm constantly reminded of wealth and abundance.

I remember that money flows to me from various sources, both known and unknown, with ease and happiness.

Then something extraordinary occurs—the money begins to flow, sales increase, and unexpected financial opportunities emerge. Give it a try.

Remembering wealth can take various forms. You can start with a simple goal: "I remember I have $10,000 ($100,000 or $1,000,000) in my bank account now." You don't need to know the how; just begin remembering that you have it. Utilize the techniques mentioned earlier, and then release it, allowing the universe to work its magic.

If you have a specific date in mind, you can remember from the future. For example, "On February 28, 2024, I have $10,000 ($100,000 or $1,000,000) extra from sources, known and unknown. I remember I so appreciate my extra $10,000" (dated December 20, 2023). Sign it.

You can also write a card or note to yourself and keep remembering that you have the desired wealth. Focus on the feeling of genuine pleasure and gratitude for having this extra money, knowing that you don't need it but truly appreciate it.

The law of detachment is very powerful. The less attached you are to the outcome, the more effective the process becomes. This is precisely why the Remembering Technique can yield such remarkable results.

Summary – Cultivating Wealth through Remembering

1. **Initiating Wealth Consciousness:** Embracing the concept that wealth is an energy and recognizing it as an infinite resource is the initial step in this process. To manifest wealth through remembering, you can utilize a tangible reminder, such as a high-denomination banknote or a symbolic item resembling money. This helps reinforce the idea of your financial potential.

2. **Remembering and Affirmation of Wealth:** Integrate representations of money into your daily environment, whether it's in your home, car, or office. The consistent presence of these symbols reinforces your belief in the abundance of wealth in your life. Through regular exposure to these reminders, you condition your mind to welcome and attract financial prosperity.

3. **The Power of Subconscious Reinforcement:** Seeing representations of wealth on a regular basis ingrains a sense of abundance in your subconscious. Whether it's discovering a $50 note in your cupboard or stumbling upon one in your car, these reminders serve as cues for your financial prosperity. This consistent reinforcement plays a crucial role in reshaping your beliefs and attitudes toward money and wealth.

4. **Transforming Beliefs about Wealth:** The technique of remembering wealth encompasses more than mere

visualization of money; it involves a transformation in your perception and relationship with money. Shifting your mindset from one of scarcity to abundance is the key to attracting greater wealth into your life.

5. **Consistency in Practice:** As with any form of mental training, consistency plays a vital role in the effectiveness of this practice. Incorporate the habit of remembering and integrating symbols of wealth into your daily routine. The regularity of this reinforcement is essential for transitioning your mindset from scarcity to abundance.

In conclusion, Chapter 10 provides practical strategies for using the art of remembering and symbolic representation to attract wealth and transform one's relationship with money. It emphasizes the importance of consistency in incorporating these practices into daily life to shift from a mindset of scarcity to one of abundance. This chapter serves as a guide to creating an environment and mindset that align with financial prosperity and a more abundant life.

Chapter Eleven

REMEMBERING THE PERFECT RELATIONSHIP

Chapter Eleven explores the deeply personal journey of relationships and the art of remembering in this context. It explores how past relationship experiences can be valuable lessons and contribute to the creation of a clear vision for future connections.

This chapter emphasizes the significance of specificity in visualizing an ideal partner and how positive and detailed thinking can pave the way for manifesting meaningful relationships that align with our values and desires.

It highlights the power of mental clarity and intention in shaping our personal experiences and intimate connections with others.

Long ago, I went through a profound learning experience in a past relationship, and it has since allowed me to remember what I truly desire in the perfect partnership from my memories.

Lessons from the Past

We often hold vivid memories of our failures, embarrassments, and past horrors. But what if we choose to transform these memories into valuable lessons? I have a personal story to share about a lesson I learned and how I turned that lesson into a memory that eventually led to the manifestation of my wonderful partner.

Having acquired new techniques related to the Law of Attraction, I began actively applying them and experimenting with various methods to manifest my desires.

I asked myself: what am I missing? I'm young and single, and I desire a relationship. Despite my self-assuredness, I acknowledged that there might be more to learn. To gain clarity, I turned to mind mapping, sitting down to put my thoughts on paper:

Good-looking/attractive, friendly, nice, loyal, committed, affectionate, no financial strings, local, available/single, we get along, happy, easy to be with—I like him!

I signed the mind map and tucked it away. It wasn't long before my dream guy appeared. He embodied all the qualities I had listed—sleek, good-looking, kind, loyal, affectionate, friendly, local, single, easy to be with, and happy. I was absolutely thrilled.

The only problem was he was a tomcat.

This cat showed up unexpectedly, possessing all the qualities I had listed, but not quite in the human form I had envisioned. It was a humorous twist, but it drove home the lesson I had learned.

What did I do differently next time?

Firstly, I remembered in list form what I really wanted, what was important to me:

- Loyal
- Honest
- Caring
- Thoughtful
- Fun
- Happy
- Financially Secure
- Generous
- Calm
- Similar Interests
- Helpful
- Sexy

I carefully outlined each facet, from his physical traits to his moral values, underscoring their importance. This encompassed his love for travel, his proficiency in the bedroom, his demeanor, and even his baggage, ensuring he carried no emotional burdens or lingering attachments to previous relationships, etc.

I remembered exactly what I wanted, and was very specific. I had been on my own for nearly two years. I loved it; the freedom, the space, the healing. Then, in the summer of 2018, I revisited my list, remembering exactly what I wanted. I had a vivid memory of the kind of man I sought. Someone who, like me, had faced challenges and longed to meet a special person.

I remembered it so clearly.

On August 8, 2018, precisely at 9 a.m., I stood at the pedestrian crossing, pressing the button at the traffic light. In that moment, I distinctly remembered that the time had come. It felt effortless, and my desire was clear—I wanted it now. After pushing the button and crossing the street, I continued with my morning routine, grabbing my coffee before heading back to work, and I simply let go of the thought.

I was alone in the shop that day, and it happened to be quite a busy one. At around 1 p.m., a friendly gentleman recommended by another jeweler arrived. He had captivating eyes, dressed casually, and exuded a sense of calm. However, I was preoccupied with work, so I politely asked if he could return later. To my surprise, he agreed and came back as I had suggested, at 3 p.m. Over the next three hours, we engaged in conversation, sharing stories and experiences.

Despite my initial nervousness about dating anyone, I found him to be genuinely nice and easy to be around. We agreed that he would return on Friday to address the jewelry repairs he needed.

We have now been together for five and a half wonderful years, experiencing a level of happiness and contentment that matches my fondest memories and desires. Our relationship is peaceful, harmonious, and filled with joy, just as I had remembered beforehand.

Summary – Crafting the Ideal Relationship through Remembering

1. **Learning from the Past:** The path to finding the ideal relationship often starts with learning from past experiences. My journey towards discovering true love began with a humorous yet enlightening incident involving my pet cat. This experience emphasized the significance of being specific and precise about my genuine desires in a partner.

2. **Remembering Your Ideal Partner:** After the tomcat incident, I fine-tuned my approach. I placed my emphasis on qualities that held profound importance: loyalty, honesty, compassion, thoughtfulness, a sense of fun, financial stability, generosity, and physical attractiveness. I meticulously envisioned every aspect of my dream partner, from their physical features to their moral values and emotional readiness.

3. **Manifesting a Perfect Match:** I remembered my perfect partner in detail while enjoying my independence but being clear about my desires. In the summer of 2018, with a vivid mental image of the man I hoped to meet, I felt ready. Then, I encountered someone who closely matched my criteria. We connected instantly, shared stories, and discovered deep compatibility.

4. **The Power of Specific Remembering:** This experience underscored the potency of specific remembering.

Clarity about your desires in a relationship can seemingly prompt the universe to respond in kind. It's crucial to move beyond superficial traits and concentrate on deeper values and compatibility elements. Envision not only the person you wish to meet but also how they will harmonize with your life and values.

5. **Transforming and Reframing Past Relationships:** Reframing past relationships with a perspective of learning and growth is essential to prepare oneself for a future relationship that is healthier and more fulfilling.

6. **Continuous Remembering and Belief:** The process of finding an ideal relationship through remembering is ongoing and demands continuous belief and commitment, even when circumstances may appear challenging. Consistently remembering and reaffirming the qualities you seek in a partner will help guide your choices towards aligning with your desires.

In conclusion, Chapter 11 integrates practical strategies for attracting the ideal romantic partner through the power of remembering. It emphasizes the importance of learning from past relationship experiences and transforming them into a clear vision for future connections. Specificity in visualizing the desired partner and maintaining positive, detailed thinking are key themes. This chapter highlights the significance of mental clarity and intention in shaping successful relationships, emphasizing the transformative potential of remembering in matters of the heart.

Chapter Twelve

REMEMBERING
FOR OTHERS

Chapter Twelve delves into the influential potential of positive remembering for others. This exploration goes beyond personal goals, revealing how intentional remembering can profoundly impact the lives of those around us.

Whether envisioning success in their pursuits or contributing to their well-being, this chapter uncovers the interconnected nature of our intentions and the experiences of others. Practical examples and techniques are presented, showcasing the generous power of remembering to enhance the lives of individuals within our communities.

Remembering for Others

Can I positively influence others through remembering? Absolutely! You can direct your thoughts towards positive outcomes for them, such as having an excellent day or achieving success in a sports match (football, netball, hockey).

Recall the healing journey of the little girl supported by her family. Extend your remembering to their good health—the potential is limitless. Here are a few examples to contemplate or incorporate into your practice: I utilized this technique with my daughter, yielding remarkable results. On numerous occasions, she attained the prestigious 'man of the match' status.

Have you ever thought of someone or something, and then suddenly, it appeared? This technique operates similarly but with a positive twist. Consistently visualize favorable outcomes for others, as I did with my daughter. I delighted in hearing about her wonderful school days and how things consistently worked out for her. Despite encountering challenges, these positive intentions consistently led to things working out for her.

Summary – Remembering Success for Others and Harnessing Collective Memory

1. **Expanding the Power of Remembering:** The transformative power of remembering isn't confined to personal aspirations; it extends to remembering positive outcomes for others. Whether it involves picturing success in a sports match, wishing a swift recovery for someone unwell, or simply desiring happiness for a loved one, the art of remembering can wield a profound impact on shaping positive outcomes in the lives of others.

2. **The Ripple Effect of Positive Remembering:** In my journey of remembering success for others, a poignant example involved supporting my daughter in her sports matches. By vividly recalling her triumphs, the impact was extraordinary, demonstrating the potential of this practice. This approach not only contributed to her success but also cultivated a driven and focused yet serene disposition in her achievements.

3. **Manifesting Positive Experiences for Loved Ones:** Much like manifesting positive outcomes for ourselves, we hold the power to do the same for those in our circles. By vividly envisioning a future filled with success and well-being for others, we become catalysts for positive change in their lives. This practice extends beyond specific visualizations, encompassing a broader sense of promoting overall well-being and success for those we care about.

4. **Techniques for Remembering for Others:** Begin by establishing a clear intention for the person you want to support—whether it's their recovery from an illness, success in an exam, or simply having a great day. Share this intention with someone or write it down to reinforce it. Throughout the day, hold this memory in your mind, gently focusing on the positive outcome you're remembering for them.

5. **Personal Experience and Growth:** This practice became a regular part of my life, particularly in my interactions with my daughter. Remembering her having a great day at school would often materialize into reality. It taught me the power of extending positive remembering beyond myself, creating a ripple effect of positivity and success.

6. **The Impact of Positive Remembering on Relationships:** By practicing this technique, we not only contribute to the well-being of others but also strengthen our relationships with them. It fosters a sense of connectedness and empathy, as we actively contribute to others' happiness and success.

In conclusion, Chapter 12 weaves together practical techniques and personal anecdotes, showcasing the transformative influence of remembering for the benefit of others. It emphasizes how visualizing positive outcomes can tangibly impact their lives, illustrating the profound interconnectedness between our intentions and the well-being of those in our circle. This chapter serves as a compelling guide, showcasing the expansive reach of the Remembering Technique and underscoring its potential to bring about positive change beyond individual aspirations.

Chapter Thirteen

POSITIVITY: LET GO OF NEGATIVITY

Chapter Thirteen navigates the transformative journey of embracing positivity and discarding negativity through the art of remembering. The chapter serves as a guide, leading readers through the process of reshaping internal dialogues and perceptions. By emphasizing the profound impact of a positive mindset on life's trajectory, it explores strategies to break free from entrenched negative thought patterns.

This exploration not only underscores the importance of maintaining optimism but also provides practical techniques for navigating life's challenges with resilience.

It's a journey towards a more joyful, fulfilling existence, underpinned by the power of positive remembering and the ability to transform our reality from within.

Remembering to Align/Be Positive

Raising your vibration is a powerful tool for transformation. It doesn't mean we aren't human, or that we don't have contrast in our lives; it's how we deal with it when it arrives that matters.

Become aware of the contrast, then intentionally elevate your vibration. By connecting with your higher self and embracing a higher vibration, you open yourself to new realms of possibilities.

When studying the Law of Attraction, I used to struggle with this problem often. How do you accomplish this when you are so in your head, replaying all the things you've got to do and trying to figure out the solution to this and that? The negative loop seems endless, trapping you in a continuous cycle of unfavorable thoughts and emotions.

In the beginning, I struggled with changing this aspect, as I had mastered the art of dwelling in negative emotions. I was proficient at making myself feel out of control and down. Not quite depression, but not a great place. How could one possibly feel good amidst the chaos of feeling lost, hurt, angry, confused, and unsure?

The solution was always remarkably simple but incredibly challenging to do.

I found comfort in the familiar feeling of desperation. It was an old emotional response I used to beat myself up with, but it didn't lead me anywhere positive. Instead, it intensified my negative feelings. The constant cycle of doom and gloom in my thoughts resulted in heightened levels of anxiety, trauma, and nervousness, turning me into a literal nervous wreck.

Shifting your focus to more positive things initiates change—it's a fundamental law. What you focus on is what you attract, making your thoughts immensely influential in shaping your reality.

Remembering that today is a great day automatically sets the intention for it to be so. Your memory is a powerful tool, and understanding that higher vibrations and positive feelings can move mountains allows you to decide to remember right now. You can change in this very second.

When contrast arises—and it will, as you created it—you can release it in the same moment. Just remember that it all worked out for you and more. Remember that you have the solution.

Always remember what's best for you.

All it takes is a breath. Inhale deeply, consciously shifting your state to one that is productive and positive, not necessarily focused on the issues. I begin by expressing gratitude for something small, and actively seek out things to appreciate. It works wonders.

Here is another way to change your state/mood/feelings.

In moments of panic, worry, or frustration, shifting my state is remarkably simple. I remember the blueness of the sky, or the dryness of the day. I remember that I am healthy and happy. Gratitude floods in for all that I have. I remember that I hold all the answers; I simply need to recall them.

Remember today is a good day, and so is tomorrow; your life is inherently good. Life itself is good. Remind yourself of the power of choice. Remember to love every aspect of yourself today, embracing all that you are. Don't forget to request miracles and genuinely like yourself—every part of yourself. Remember that you matter.

The recall I have of today is magnificent. I was open to miracles.

I remembered experiencing miracles throughout the day—magnificent miracles. I reminisce about the happiness and positive outcomes that filled my day. What a great day.

Remembering the Fun

Why do we take life so seriously?

When did we lose touch with the joy of living and spend most of our days in a place of plain old seriousness? It's an odd place to be. What does this approach achieve? I don't mean that we shouldn't take our responsibilities seriously. I know it may sound contradictory, but consider this: Why does life have to be so boring, bland, serious, and draining? Why do we think it needs to be hard?

I recall the moment I decided to remember to break free from the old habit of worry, nerves, and a sense of dread. Despite knowing that everything can change in a heartbeat, a breath, a moment, I found myself repeatedly returning to the same old negativity. It provided comfort, a false sense of certainty. I played the victim role, clinging to excuses. But excuses for what?

For putting pressure on myself, constantly moaning and feeling like a failure.

I had mastered the art of creating a negative narrative in my mind. It was a situation of my own making. Taking responsibility for all my actions and reactions was a revelation, albeit a heavy responsibility. Once I acknowledged that I had created this reality, the question arose: How do I uncreate it?

The solution was surprisingly simple. I shifted my focus from the current moment and immediately recalled that I was in a better place than I had ever imagined. I remembered the multitude of solutions available to me. I remembered that I possess everything needed. I embraced the memory of the new me—someone who is funny, happy, light, positive, creative, relaxed, calm, serene, peaceful, successful, and full of fun. My expectations shifted to anticipating only the very best.

Remember to Love Yourself. How?

There are several ways you can do this. We are often our harshest critics, and we criticize ourselves all the time. Why not start remembering all the good things about ourselves? Begin modestly if needed; appreciate features like your captivating eyes or your talent for baking great cakes. Remember the joy you derive from simple things, such as the comfort in your favorite shoes, or the pleasure of walking your dog. Then remember new things to love. Remember the kindness you show yourself, cherish the evolving version of you, and embrace your success and excellent health. Remember you love yourself, and how much you love being with others. Remember the great things others see in you. Remember and celebrate these qualities, cultivating an expanding love for the person you are both inside and out.

Remember You Are Worthy

Do you want the very best in life?

If you want to experience a life filled with optimal health, abundant wealth, and fulfilling relationships, change is imperative. The question then arises: How do you embark on this transformative journey?

In your new life, focus on remembering your worthiness of the very best—optimal health, boundless wealth, and fulfilling relationships. Strengthen this belief through repetition. Record affirmations, listen to them twice daily, write them down, and display them prominently. The more you encounter these reminders, the more they become ingrained truths.

Remembering Conflict

In situations where a positive outcome may seem uncertain, you still have a choice. Remember to visualize a positive resolution that benefits everyone involved. Picture yourself shaking hands or reaching an agreement where everyone is content. Maintain this positive image in your mind.

In a real-life example, a friend faced a challenging court situation. Rather than dwelling on the impossibility of winning, they chose to remember a positive outcome. They remembered everyone involved shaking hands and resolving the situation, with a positive outcome for everyone.

Shortly before the court date, an amicable solution was found, and all parties involved shook hands, successfully avoiding the legal proceedings. This serves as a reminder that you, too, can influence positive outcomes by consistently remembering and focusing on a harmonious resolution for everyone.

Summary – Embracing Positivity and Transforming Negative Experiences

1. **Aligning with Positivity:** Embracing a positive mindset is essential for personal growth. Challenges are inevitable, but our response to them determines our growth. Remembering to connect with positivity and higher vibrations can reshape experiences and create opportunities. The key is to be aware of negativity and deliberately choose to elevate your vibration.

2. **Changing Your Inner Narrative:** Overcoming negative thought loops is a significant challenge many of us face. Transitioning from despair to hope requires a conscious emphasis on positive aspects, reshaping your perception of reality. A straightforward affirmation, such as "Today is a great day," can establish a powerful intention for positivity.

3. **Finding Joy and Lightness in Life:** Life doesn't have to be a continuous stream of serious and draining events. Introducing elements of fun and lightness can make a substantial difference. Empower yourself by breaking away from patterns of worry and dread. Remember, you have the ability to reshape your narrative and embrace a more joyful, positive outlook.

4. **Transforming Past Memories:** Negative past experiences can often define us. Choose to remember these events differently by focusing on positive outcomes or neutralizing their emotional charge. Transforming

memories in this way facilitates the release of old, unhelpful emotions and initiates a healing process.

5. **Self-Forgiveness and Healing:** In dealing with negative memories, practicing self-forgiveness is vital. It's not about forgetting what happened but releasing the emotional hold it has on you. Each time you revisit a negative memory, consciously choose to remember it differently, focusing on forgiveness and healing.

6. **Practicing Consistency and Repetition:** Like any skill, maintaining a consistent practice of positive remembering and memory transformation can be challenging yet rewarding. With strong motivation, this process becomes an integral part of your life's journey.

7. **Empowering Yourself and Others:** Your journey of positivity and transformation isn't just for your benefit—it extends to others around you. By adopting a positive mindset and transforming your experiences, you positively influence those nearby, contributing to a more joyful and harmonious environment.

In conclusion, Chapter 13 integrates strategies for maintaining a positive mindset, transforming negative experiences, and emphasizing the importance of self-forgiveness and consistent practice. This chapter serves as a guide to illuminating the path to embracing positivity, releasing negativity, and harnessing the power of remembering to enhance personal well-being and contribute positively to the lives of those around us.

Chapter Fourteen

REMEMBERING
EXAM RESULTS

Chapter Fourteen takes a hands-on approach to the practical applications of the Remembering Technique. It sheds light on how this method can be pivotal in achieving desired outcomes in specific situations like exams and personal challenges.

This chapter navigates through the extraordinary capacity of the mind, showcasing its ability to shape reality through focused intention and visualization. By transforming our approach to memory and anticipation, significant impacts on performance and outcomes emerge, spanning from academic success to overcoming personal barriers.

Through a blend of real-life examples and insightful strategies, this chapter provides a road map for using the power of remembering to not only envision but also actualize the results we seek in various aspects of our lives.

In our linear world, education often follows a structured path, emphasizing the use of memory. Students are taught what they have to remember so that they can go into an exam, and come out showing the world that they turned up, did the work, and now can recall the information verbatim.

Is this system outdated? Who knows? It's not for me to comment or form an opinion. What I do know is that billions of people have relied on this technique for centuries.

Success breeds success, and now we can apply this technique in a different context—using it to create the life of our dreams.

This includes exams; test it with anything you actually want to achieve. The question is, how do you change a rigid system? Here's how:

Have your goal firmly in mind, whether it's achieving top results in qualifications, earning a first honors degree, excelling in a piano or ballet assessment, succeeding in an audition, passing your driving test, or obtaining certification in a new career or technique. The possibilities are endless. (**Note: We offer Remembering Technique certification to effortlessly open up a whole new career for you.**)

Good, we now know where you are and what you want.

You've already been engaged in studying and testing yourself with memory cards; you have been doing this for some time now. Let's now extend this practice into the future.

You've learned your information, you've loved or hated the journey, and now you have this wealth of new knowledge. How do you show the world and save your nerves?

Firstly, decide that you want to do this. Determine the outcome you desire—whether it's all As, first-class honors, or just a pass. This choice is yours, and recognizing the leverage it provides is crucial.

Do you want this to work for you? If the answer is yes, you are halfway there. If the answer is no, revisit your "Why" again.

Remember, repetition is key, just like when you were a child learning to walk, tie your shoelaces, or read.

Apply the same enthusiasm; the mind thrives on positivity. It will always work to steer you away from pain. Let's work with it to save time and accelerate your results.

Your exam or event will have a date or deadline. Brilliant—the mind thrives on a deadline. Now, write in a diary, journal, on cards, or record your desired outcome. Don't forget to do this as soon as you know the date; on that day, write this and put at the bottom of the page the actual date you remembered it. It's delightful to look back and see when you actually remembered your outcome. Use this as a model:

Date: May 5, 2025, Piano exam level one (Remembered Jan 1, 2025, signed DL)

I remember feeling calm, happy, and thrilled after successfully completing my piano assessment for Level 1. The experience was effortless, and I genuinely enjoyed it. I practiced diligently, both physically and in my mind. (It is proven that you can achieve as much success visually imagining doing a process as well as physically doing it. Use every approach available to you.)

Now pretend it's May 5, 2025. You feel so good; you just sit there saying to yourself or writing or reading out loud:

Today is May 5, 2025, and what a fantastic day it is! I feel incredibly calm, relaxed, serene, and happy. Taking my piano exam on May 5, 2025, was such a joyous experience. Everything flowed seamlessly, and I remember so clearly the readiness and ease with which I approached my practice and the exam. It was truly a great day.

I embraced a serene calmness, confident in playing each note with precision. The love I have for the piano and the music naturally emanated in my performance, and I knew the examiner would feel it too. I was so happy; it was undoubtedly a good exam—the best. I achieved so much, and I cherished every moment of this joyous day.

Another example is school exams. This is how I would write it for my exams:

Date: August 5, 2024 – exam results day for English GCSE (only an example date)

I remember with such clarity what a great day it was. I was with my friends; we were so excited.

Secondary school is over; we are loving the summer and looking forward to our sixth form.

I recall the quiet excitement I felt when I took the exam. I was extremely calm and happy. The day of the exam was so easy; it felt as if I were gliding through the exam and every lesson I learned, from reading the paper clearly to following my well-practiced plan.

As I sat in the exam, I understood the questions. I knew the answers. Completing each question, the right answers seamlessly flowed to me. Writing flowed effortlessly, in context and in good time. Without second-guessing myself, I allowed everything I had learned to flow through my pen. The process felt natural, and I experienced a profound sense of peace and calm. It was a beautiful opportunity to showcase my love for English and demonstrate how much I had learned. The exam paper felt as if it were written for me, and every answer was at my fingertips. (Remembered Jan 9, 2024, DL)

Remembering New Memories

Old Memories into New

We all have them—memories that haunt us, events that felt unfair or wrong. Habitually, we replay these moments, reliving our fears, upsets, and woes. But what's the result? We carry guilt and unhappiness, and find ourselves stuck in repeated patterns, often without understanding why.

We can allow these memories to continue defining us, or we can choose to change them. We can remember them as they were, or we can choose to reshape them into how we'd like them to be, thus changing our beliefs as well. You have the power to change what no longer serves you. As you change, so does your life. It's a natural law: where you focus, you will achieve. The simplest way is to remember that you already possess what you seek.

This implies that old emotions can be transformed—not to erase what happened, but to clear away the old, unhelpful emotions associated with it. You have the power to neutralize the emotion; you can choose to remember without emotional charge and extract the lesson.

Holding onto resentment is like drinking poison and expecting the other person to suffer. The negative emotions associated with such thoughts may go unnoticed by the person involved. If you choose not to forget the harm caused, forgiving yourself is a liberating action. Regardless of the other person's continued behavior, the act of self-forgiveness releases you from the burden. Simply remember that you have forgiven yourself; it doesn't require a specific reason or action, just the acknowledgment that you have let it go.

Remembering to forgive yourself is a powerful act of releasing guilt, judgment, and wasted emotions. Holding onto these negative feelings serves no one—especially not you. It doesn't necessarily mean you have to reconnect with the person involved. By letting go of guilt, judgment, and unnecessary emotions, you free yourself from the grip of resentment and anger. Remembering that you've forgiven yourself is a compassionate and healing step towards your own well-being.

Whenever you find yourself replaying a negative memory, emotion, or thought, remember to change it. Choose to change that memory and, most importantly, remember to forgive yourself.

I cannot tell you how much better you will feel, not only about yourself, but your day, and even your life.

Consistency is key; keep reminding yourself of this new way because you've been used to the old patterns for a long time.

Summary – Transforming Exam Experiences and Remembering New Memories

1. **Embracing the Exam Journey:** In our linear world, where education often relies on memory and repetition, harnessing the power of remembering can be transformative, especially for exams. Whether it's academic tests, music exams, or professional certifications, setting clear goals is the first step. Remember your success vividly: see yourself achieving top grades or excelling in your field. This remembering can redefine your approach to learning and testing.

2. **Remembering Academic Success:** For example, if you're preparing for a piano assessment, remember after the event, not only the day of the exam but also the process leading up to it. Visualize yourself playing each piece flawlessly, feeling confident and at ease. Such detailed remembering can significantly impact your performance and mindset.

3. **Reimagining Past Memories:** We often carry burdensome memories that shape our fears and self-doubt. By transforming these memories, you can change the associated emotions and beliefs. Remember these events differently, focusing on positive outcomes or neutralizing negative emotions. This practice can free you from past constraints and open new possibilities for personal growth.

4. **Repetition and Consistency:** Mastering the art of remembering for exams, like any skill, requires practice. Consistently recall your successes, embedding these positive outcomes deep into your subconscious. This repetitive process enhances your confidence and readies you for the actual exam.

5. **Forging a Positive Future:** As you continue to use the technique of remembering, you'll notice an increased ability to recall information and maintain composure under pressure. Whether it's recalling exam answers or overcoming performance anxiety, your transformed memories become a powerful tool for achieving success.

6. **Remembering New Memories:** In every aspect of life, from exams to personal challenges, the Remembering Technique can be a transformative tool. It offers a fresh perspective, converting anxiety into anticipation and fundamentally reshaping the way one perceives and engages with the world.

In summary, Chapter 14 blends practical approaches to memory techniques for exams and personal challenges with transformative insights into reshaping past experiences and memories. This chapter serves as a comprehensive guide to harnessing the power of remembering and memory, empowering you to achieve academic success, foster personal growth, and cultivate a positive outlook on life.

Chapter Fifteen

LOST ITEMS

Chapter Fifteen invites us into the fascinating world of rediscovering and reclaiming lost items through the art of remembering.

Here, we delve into the effectiveness of focused memory and visualization as powerful tools in locating misplaced or lost belongings. This chapter explores various mental strategies and techniques that aid in jogging our memory, offering clarity and insight in moments of forgetfulness. Through personal anecdotes and practical tips, what follows is a demonstration of how harnessing our cognitive abilities can transform the often-frustrating experience of losing items into an opportunity to enhance memory skills and bring a sense of control and order to our daily lives.

The Lost Earrings

Do you ever have those days when you put something down and then can't find it? You can't remember where you put it!

Here is how you remember for lost items.

One day at home, I had a pair of earrings that I was excited to wear. I thought I had put them in a packet with a necklace I wanted to wear, and couldn't believe it when I checked my bag for the earrings, but found only the necklace.

I checked where I last had them, but still no earrings. I had time, so I wasn't too worried; they would turn up eventually.

Then I simply decided that by 11 a.m. that morning, I would remember where they were. I wrote it down and even discussed it with a friend, mentioning that I remembered where the earrings were and would find them by 11 a.m. (it was 9 a.m.).

I carried on with my day, handling mail and sorting out problems. Not long after, I felt an urge to tidy up a certain area of my house. It wasn't directly where I had been with the earrings and necklace, but it was nearby.

Within five minutes of starting to tidy and clear the area, lo and behold, the earrings were found. It was 10:55 a.m.— what a result! I was elated. I had no idea how the earrings ended up where I found them, but it didn't matter; they were found.

You, too, can do this. This is what I did:

> Challenge: I remembered clearly that by 11 a.m., I had found my 18ct gold earrings, easily and happily.

> Result: At 10:55 a.m., the earrings were found in a box, not far from where I thought I had left them but couldn't find earlier.

As you cultivate the habit of remembering to find things, it's astonishing how effortlessly it works. Briefly thinking about something will prompt recall. You will start to find things with ease and little effort.

Summary –
Mastering Memory in Daily Life

1. **The Journey Begins:** Remembering to start is crucial. This straightforward action serves as the cornerstone of commitment and discipline. While it may seem minor, it marks the inception of transformation. Keep in mind that this is your journey towards a successful life—a chance to reshape your identity, acknowledge your capabilities, and strive for your aspirations.

2. **Embracing Clarity and Responsibility:** Recognizing your current position is the first step towards change. It entails moving away from a mindset of assigning blame to embracing a proactive approach to success. Pledge to maintain this consciousness daily, as it forms a crucial part of the life you are constructing. Keep in mind, it's all about your journey and personal development.

3. **Focusing on Desired Outcomes:** Often, we dwell on what we don't want, leading to negativity and complaints. Instead, focus your energy on expressing and recalling your genuine desires. This transition holds immense power, influencing your choices and actions. Remember, the manner in which you visualize your future molds every moment of your life. Choose ease and joy in this transformative process.

4. **Finding Your Unique Method:** The art of remembering isn't one-size-fits-all. Discover what resonates with you, be it words, imagery, or feelings. Then, hold onto them in your memory.

In conclusion, Chapter 15 explores the intriguing prospect of employing memory and remembering techniques to locate lost items. It provides practical steps for setting intentions, reinforcing them, and remaining open to intuitive guidance. This chapter serves as a guide to transforming the typically stressful experience of losing items into an opportunity to harness the power of the mind, demonstrating how a shift in mindset can lead to surprising and delightful discoveries.

SUMMARY
CHAPTER

1. Remember to get started! This might seem simple, but simplicity should not deter us from taking action. This is the point where commitment and discipline come into play.

2. Remember to gain clarity about where you are. Acknowledging your present circumstances and embracing responsibility transforms your mindset from a culture of blame to one of success.

   This is something we need to commit to every day; remember, it's your journey to success. Remember who you are, what you have, and what you desire.

3. Remember to ask for what you desire. It's common to focus on what we don't want, moaning about this and that. However, the effort spent on identifying what we don't want can be redirected toward asking and achieving what we truly desire.

   Continuously remember what you desire, and this will influence your decisions and actions. Your future memories will shape each moment of your life. The process can be as hard or as easy as you choose. My recommendation (and I know it works) is to ask for the easy way—it's kinder, more enjoyable, and you don't need to work too hard.

4. Remember to try different methods and see what resonates with you. Whether you choose to remember, recall, or memorize your future, the choice is yours. As I mentioned earlier, memorization can be surprisingly easy, as demonstrated by the accomplishments of memory experts with complex challenges like Pi.

You can do the same, whether you choose words, pictures, characters, cards, mirrors, or journals/diaries.

When connecting with our inner child, our fun self, we open the gateway for the best to emerge—our inner being, higher self, and subconscious mind.

It doesn't matter what label you assign to it, this inner force only desires the best for you. The key is to engage with it, communicate, and establish a connection. Like any skill, practice is essential, much like learning to walk or ride a bike. It takes time.

Can you speed up that time and learning process? You most certainly can! For more detailed information, please visit my website.

5. Remember to keep doing it! Repetition is the key to mastery. Always bear in mind: discipline yields results.

It may seem like the easiest thing in the world to do, yet at times, it can be the most challenging.

If your "Why" is significant enough, the process becomes effortless; it requires no assistance. Remember to follow the steps outlined in this book and open your mind to this new world.

6. Remember to think big! How big? The size of your aspirations is entirely up to you. Perhaps you'd like to begin by testing the system on achieving an effortless day, a holiday, or a journey.

Over time, you will have effortlessly and easily changed your beliefs, and remember, your beliefs define your world.

When I began practicing the Remembering Technique, I also started listening to my homemade voice memo on my iPhone. I remembered that I was a great author. I remembered that I was a bestseller, and now I am!

Was I born an author? Absolutely not. In fact, my old mindset revolved around disliking English. And I hated paperwork! If you were to ask anyone who knows me, completing paperwork was my greatest nightmare; I would go to great lengths to avoid writing.

Over time I have changed that view. My paperwork is always organized.

For example, I used to procrastinate with my accounts, leaving them until the last minute. Hunting for the necessary paperwork was a genuine nightmare; I struggled to recall where I had placed things and had difficulty remembering specific events I needed to explain.

The pressure was immense, and it was an experience I did not enjoy. Finding the money I needed to pay added to the strain, and my stress was off the charts.

Do I have stress now? Absolutely. It's part of life. However, as soon as I recognize one of my stress-inducing behaviors, I make a conscious effort to change it.

I began remembering the desired outcome I wanted to achieve and transform within myself. Now, not only do I submit my accounts early, but I also happily provide all the information the accountants need. It's no trouble at all, and I enjoy seeing the positive results of early submission, relieving the pressure on myself.

This didn't happen by accident. I remembered daily that I had achieved it.

I remembered in the future that I had succeeded easily, and it is easy.

7. Remember who you are. This is very important because you are special, unique, talented, and above all, because you matter. You make a difference, not only in your life but in the lives of others.

I love the movie *It's a Wonderful Life*.

If you truly want to recognize who you are and how loved you are, consider all the people around you, those you interact with, and importantly, acknowledge what you bring to their lives. There's something you do effortlessly that they can't or don't want to do, making a meaningful impact.

Now it's your turn to remember what you can do for yourself. Yes, you. You matter.

Making your life work for you means you can give so much more to others. Perhaps you'll teach them to remember who they are and the goodness, joy, and love they bring to your world.

This technique is here to help you unravel and produce the greatest secret of all—your power!

According to an old legend, three Gods observed from above, desiring to bestow infinite power upon humans. Recognizing the immense value of this gift, they decided to make it challenging to find, as they believed that humans wouldn't fully appreciate it otherwise.

In their discussion, they talked openly about where to hide it.

The first God suggested, "Let's hide it on top of the highest mountain; they won't think to look there." However, the other two Gods disagreed, expressing concern that humans would find a way to conquer the mountain, making it an unsuitable hiding place.

The second God proposed, "I think we should place it at the bottom of the ocean; it's so deep and unknown." However, the other Gods thought about it and agreed that humans would likely find a way to reach the depths of the ocean.

The third God pondered for a moment and then suggested, "I know, let's hide it within man himself; he will never think to look there."

All three Gods agreed, and that is where your power resides.

Within the pages of this book and with the Remembering Technique, you have now found your power. Use it wisely.

Use it to help yourself and others in a positive way.

This world has the potential to be a better place, regardless of where you are or your personal beliefs, religious or otherwise.

It starts today, with you remembering that it can be better.

There's a saying that goes, "How do you eat an elephant? One bite at a time." Start remembering your future now, and you'll soon see the difference!

If you feel inspired to explore more, or for further guidance to join my collective mediation for a better world, please go to my website: www.TheRemembering-Technique.com.

Integrated Summary Chapter

1. **The Initiation of Remembering:** Embarking on this journey may seem straightforward, yet it requires commitment and discipline. The simplicity of the act of remembering shouldn't undermine its necessity. This initial step of commitment is your gateway to transformation.

2. **Clarity and Ownership:** Recognizing your current position and embracing responsibility for your journey marks the shift from a blame culture to a culture of success. Every day, remember your path by acknowledging where you are and envisioning where you want to be.

3. **The Art of Desire and Intention:** Shift your focus from dwelling on the unwanted to actively seeking what you desire. This subtle yet powerful change in thought process will redefine your actions and decisions, shaping your future in every moment. Choose ease and joy on this path.

4. **Personalizing Your Approach:** Whether through words, imagery, or other mediums, find the method of remembering that resonates with you. Approach it as a playful and open dialogue with your inner self. Like any skill, it thrives on practice and exploration.

5. **Consistency in Practice:** Repetition is key to mastering the art of remembering. While it may seem simple,

maintaining this practice demands dedication. Let your strong motivation guide you to make remembering an integral part of your life.

6. **Thinking Big and Boldly:** Dare to dream without limits. Begin with manageable goals, gradually progressing to larger aspirations. My journey from a reluctant writer to a best-selling author started with remembering and reshaping my beliefs. Let this technique transform your reality. Self-Discovery and Empowerment: Acknowledge your uniqueness and the profound impact you have on both others and yourself. Reflect on your contributions, and now focus on what you can do for yourself. You are special, talented, and your journey through remembering is about unlocking your true potential.

7. **Unveiling the Hidden Power Within:** The ancient parable of gods concealing infinite power within humans serves as a profound reminder that our greatest strength resides within ourselves. The Remembering Technique, explored in this book, unveils this inner power. Utilize it wisely to enrich your own life and exert a positive influence on those around you.

8. **Continuing the Journey:** If you feel inspired to delve deeper or seek additional guidance on collective meditation, visit TheRememberingTechnique.com. Begin with small steps and witness the transformative power of remembering your future.

This integrated summary chapter brings together the core concepts of the original content while providing enhanced insights. It serves as a comprehensive guide on harnessing the power of remembering for personal growth, clarity, and transformation. It serves as a road map, encouraging readers to embrace their journey with intention, practice, and a vision of their highest potential.

ACKNOWLEDGEMENTS

This book would not have been possible without the love, support, and encouragement of several extraordinary individuals.

To my daughter, Willow, you are my constant source of inspiration and joy. Your unwavering belief in me has been my guiding light. Thank you for your patience, your laughter, and for reminding me every day of the beautiful possibilities in life.

To my partner, Nick, your steadfast support and understanding have been my rock. Thank you for always being there, for your endless encouragement, and for the countless ways you've helped me stay balanced and focused throughout this journey.

To My Mentor, Peggy, who supported me in so many ways seen and unseen, who's commitment and vision, helped bring this dream alive. Thank you from the bottom of my heart, action's speak louder than words you are the epitome of this.

To my close friends, you have been my pillars of strength. Your encouragement, wisdom, and friendship have been invaluable. Thank you for believing in me and for the many ways you've contributed to my growth both personally and professionally. Your support has meant the world to me.

Lastly, to everyone who has believed in The Remembering Technique and supported me along the way, your faith and enthusiasm have been the driving force behind this work. I am deeply grateful for each and every one of you.

With heartfelt gratitude,

ABOUT THE AUTHOR

Meet Donna, a proud mother to her beautiful daughter Willow, a dream realized against all odds.

Donna is not just a mother but an award-winning entrepreneur and an accomplished dream maker for others. She has collaborated with a top local sport personality to achieve unbelievable outcomes, such as raising a million pounds for Cancer Research and completing untested physical challenges.

Donna's remarkable journey doesn't stop there. She has helped a young girl in a wheelchair to walk, granting her full independence, and transformed the life of a single mother struggling to create a better life in a new country for herself and her children.

With a true passion for learning and a dedication to expanding the mind, Donna has committed the last 30 years to exploring and mastering techniques to enrich her own life and the lives of others.

Donna often says, "If you don't have a plan for life, life will have a plan for you. What is your plan?"

She has realized her desires time and again, from having her miracle child and escaping a toxic relationship to owning successful businesses and having a partner who loves her just the way she is.

As the creator of 'The Remembering Technique,' an effortless way to use your memory to achieve your deepest desires, Donna is here to help you reach dreams you never thought possible.

With a wealth of knowledge and a commitment to what works, Donna pushes boundaries to new limits. If you want a new life, better health, more abundance, or a fulfilling relationship, contact Donna at www.TheRememberingTechnique.com and start your journey to the life you've always dreamed of.

UNLOCK THE SECRET TO UNLEASHING YOUR NEW LIFE!

Introducing: The Remembering Technique Course

Imagine effortlessly creating the life you dream of, with clarity and precision. Picture yourself acing exams, nailing presentations, and remembering what you want and achieving it.

Welcome to the Remembering Technique Course, your gateway to mastering your future through your memory.

Why Do You Need This Course?

In our fast-paced world, memory isn't just a skill—it's a superpower. Yet, so many of us struggle with using our superpower overwhelmed by the sheer volume of information we encounter daily. What if you could turn this around? What if you could:

- **Boost Your Academic Performance**: Impress yourself and those around you as you achieve new heights of success and achievement, easily.

- **Excel in Your Career**: Stand out in meetings, enjoy your work/career, and enhance your professional reputation.

- **Improve Personal Relationships**: Being in relationships that work for you, that support and improve your life and those around you.

- **Create the New You, Your New Life**: Effortlessly being all you can be and more, in a life you choose.

What is the Remembering Technique?

The Remembering Technique is a scientifically backed method created to enhance you're your life dramatically. This isn't about rote learning or tedious repetition—it's about unlocking the natural power of your brain and to work efficiently, effortlessly, with incredible success.

What Will You Learn?

- **Future Memory Foundations**: Understand how memory works and discover techniques to change the old ways to use your memory and create your future instead.

- **Visualization Strategies**: Learn how to use imagery to make memories create your future dreams.

- **Remember a New Way**: To a life you have dreamed of.

- **Use Tools that Create Success**: Changing and reinventing your beliefs.

- **Practical Applications**: Apply these techniques in real-life scenarios to see immediate results.

What Makes Our Course Unique?

- **Proven Methods**: Developed by using remembering applications and tested on hundreds of students.

- **Interactive Learning**: Engaging exercises and activities that make learning/changing fun and effective.

- **Personalized Feedback**: Get tailored advice to hone your new remembering skills to perfection.

- **Lifetime Access**: Revisit the material anytime you need a refresher.

Hear From Our Success Stories

"Before taking the Remembering Technique Course, I was struggling to change my life. Now, I've manifested my dream home, and now live my new life, that I love, effortlessly!"

— Alison B., Retail Jeweller

"I never thought I'd be able to remember so easily a new future. This course has transformed how I live, work and succeed, it's a must for anyone serious about real change with success, easily."

— Nick G., Sales Executive

Ready to Transform Your Remembering?

Don't let another moment slip away. The ability to remember your desires effortlessly is within your reach, and it starts with the Remembering Technique Course.

Sign Up Now and Receive Exclusive Bonuses!

- **Bonus 1**: Access to our private online community for support and networking.

- **Bonus 2**: Free eBook, "Master Your New Future by Remembering: Tips and Tricks for Everyday Life".

- **Bonus 3**: Personalized remembering assessment and action plan.

Join the Remembering Revolution Today!

Curiosity piqued? Desire ignited? Your journey to an exceptional life remembered begins here. Click the link below to sign up for the Remembering Technique Course and start experiencing the benefits of a powerful remembering technique.

SIGN UP NOW

Don't just remember—excel. The Remembering Technique Course is your key to unlocking an extraordinary life. Sign up today!

NEWS FLASH !! Coming Soon. If you want to take your Remembering Technique to the next level, register your interest in The Remembering Technique – Master Class Book, not to be missed.

Printed in Great Britain
by Amazon